Sexuality and Salvation

why can't we live together?

By Steve Mallon

Foreword by Richard Holloway

Scottish
Christian PRESS

First published in Great Britain
In 2004 by Scottish Christian Press
21 Young Street
Edinburgh EH2 4HU

ISBN 190432505X

Cover design and page layout by Heather Macpherson

Printed and bound in the UK by Bookchase

Dedicated to:

Sandra Weir Mallon
1941-2001

The woman who helped me discover books and
who always believed that I could write.

Our lives begin to end the day we become silent about things that matter.

Martin Luther King, Jr

Contents

Acknowledgements

What follows is sincere and is from the heart. A book like this does not come out of a vacuum, it is an expression from within a time and place. There are so many fingerprints on this book - the problem about trying to acknowledge all of them is that I know I'm bound to forget someone. However, sincere thanks need to go to my editor, Kath Davies OBE, who worked within the limits of my ability, vocabulary and courage and helped me to find my voice. To the SCP team - Gill Cloke (I will never forget your midnight editing of my dissertation), Janet de Vigne, Christine Causer and Heather Macpherson - collectively you are one of the jewels of the Kirk.

The wider staff group of the Board of Parish Education - past and present - namely, Iain Whyte, Doug Swanney, Gillian Scott, Stewart Cutler, Jayne Scott, Dr Kathleen Rankin, Lisa Clark, Anne Houston, Samantha Stringer, Jade MacLean. You all did your bit to keep the project alive and to encourage me to see it through to completion. A special mention has to go to Robin Thomson who has worked alongside me for the last few years and whose unstinting support and enthusiasm for the tasks we share is a constant inspiration. Thank you, Robin, for being you.

Thanks go to Richard Holloway for the foreword. His writing and preaching have given people like me the confidence to look beyond what we think we know. He has been involved in my work over the years at the National Youth Assembly and in training conferences and other events. I have never left his company without feeling inspired, irritated, included and challenged and I am grateful to him for finding the time to endorse this book.

Other people to thank include John Bell - he is so horribly good at everything he does - I am thankful to him that when I told him I was going to write this book he didn't die laughing! Chris Docherty, my partner in ecumenical crime, gave encouragement throughout the life of the project. Linda Galvin, who as well as being my aunt is one of my closest friends, who never stinted in her support. My friend, Penny Forshaw who has always been there for me over the last 15 or so years. Thanks also to Marion Bell, who thought I was there to nag her to keep going through our three years of study - really it was the other way round!

A special mention has to go to Gill Scott, Lecturer at Glasgow Caledonian University. Without her this project would never really have got off the ground as she was the person who made me keep going when I was about to give up. I will never forget the first line of the email she sent me to let me know I'd gained my Master's degree, 'O ye of little faith'!

But beyond all of these people there are those whose fingerprints are more prominent but whose names can never be mentioned as it just isn't safe to do so. You know who you are. I hope I have used your words well. Forgive me if I haven't. Rest assured, your witness, your pain, your tears and your joys do not go unnoticed by God. Today the Church is not worthy of your faith and commitment. But one day, a better day, things will change.

Steve Mallon
Edinburgh, January 2004

Foreword

by Richard Holloway
Writer, Broadcaster and former Bishop of Edinburgh

Any religion that claims to be in possession of a revelation from God is going to have a problem with history. To put it simply, it is always going to be a question of the immovable object meeting the irresistible force. Religion, or the God who lies behind it, is the immovable object, and history, caught in its endless flux of change, is the irresistible force. There are usually two sources of conflict in the clash between religion and human history, one epistemological, the other sociological. That awkward word 'epistemology' is from the Greek and it has to do with knowledge or what is claimed as knowledge. The classic example of an epistemological or knowledge conflict between religion and history is, no, not Darwin, but Copernicus. It's old hat to remind people that the cosmology of the Bible is based on classical astronomy, in which the earth is the centre of a tiny, three-decker universe, with everything in the heavens going round us, in more ways than one. I suspect that the really interesting point here is not that the Biblical writers invented or had this view of the cosmos revealed to them, but that it was the prevailing view in the ancient cultures of which they were a part. That's probably why most of the great creation myths of the ancient religions, including Judaism and its daughter Christianity, are broadly similar.

The difficulty arises when you associate the going view not with the current state of human knowledge, but with a fixed revelation from God. If you believe God has told you that the sun goes round the earth, what do you do when you discover that it's the other way round? There are at least two things you can do. You can simply refuse to accept the new knowledge. Lots of religious people do that with all sorts of new discoveries. They just opt out of history. To do that effectively, however, you really have to isolate and insulate yourselves in a cultural ghetto away from the flow of human history, a bit the way Hasidic Jews or Amish Christians do. It is, I suppose, one way to live, but it does not seem to be attractive to most people.

The second, more painful and strenuous response, is to develop a theology of interpretation that allows you to adapt your religious beliefs to new knowledge. However you do it, it is going to involve you in saying that humanity brings as much into the religious equation as it gets out of it. In other words, there's as much of humanity in religion as there is of divinity. And this makes perfect sense. Even if you believe in a God who is revealed to humanity, it is not hard to accept that the human end of that equation is bound to affect the way the revelation is received and understood. We never get God neat, as it were. We only get God through the agency of our humanity, and we all know how easy it is to get in our own way in all sorts of relationships and mess them up. That's why theologians spend a lot of time trying to figure out what, in the revelation they have to work on, comes from God and what comes from us. Broadly speaking, we've been quite good at that in recent centuries, which is why most of the old conflicts between religion and science are handled with greater ease today and very few theologians see any fundamental conflict between the two ways of looking at the world. So far, so straightforward, though we must never forget what a war it was at the time.

The real conflict between religion and human history has now shifted from the epistemological to the sociological realm, from claims about the structure of the universe to claims about the structure of human relationships. In other words, from astronomy to human sexuality. But the conflicts have enormous similarities. This time round it is not an ancient astronomical theory that is in conflict with history and the new knowledge it brings, it is an ancient theory of human relationships. The revealed religions inherited from their culture of origin an essentially patriarchal view of relationships, heavily dominated by male heterosexual attitudes. This is hardly surprising, since that's the way the world was organised for so long. But you only have to think about the recent struggle between this traditional way of looking at the relationship between the sexes and the way an educated and liberated woman would look at it today to see the vast gulf between them. The question theologians had to grapple with was not unlike the one Copernicus presented them with: If you believe that God has told you that women are inferior to men, what do you do when you discover that they're not? Well, you do more or less what was done with the conflict over the position of the earth in the cosmos. You either opt out of history or you negotiate. That's what theologians have been doing for centuries and it's why, contrary to the tradition of 2000 years, women are getting ordained as ministers in Christianity and as rabbis in Judaism in increasing numbers.

But here we go again. This time, as anyone who reads the papers will know, the conflict is over human sexuality. You won't be surprised to hear that the same old responses are being played out, with some people saying the issue was settled 3000 years ago in Leviticus, so they refuse to discuss it; and others saying, however wearily, let's negotiate, let's think our way theologically through the conflict the way we've always done. If you are still with me you will probably have guessed by now that I am about to commend this book precisely because it is designed to help you do just that, to get you thinking theologically about the hot button issue of our day in Christianity: human sexuality. It is carefully and bravely written to get you thinking and talking about an issue that threatens to tear Christianity apart. We've been here before, of course, but that's what happens when believers choose to live out their faith not parked in dry dock, but in the surging flood waters of time. Happy swimming.

Introduction

A *world* gone mad?

'Religious leaders have spoken out against government plans to allow gays, lesbians and co-habiting couples to adopt children. Michael Scott-Joynt, the Rt Rev the Lord Bishop of Winchester, Peter Smith, the Roman Catholic Archbishop of Cardiff, Indarjit Singh, editor of the Sikh Messenger and Iqbal AKM Sacranie OBE, Secretary General of the Muslim Council of Britain have joined forces. They added their voices to the opposition facing the government in the House of Lords today when a new Bill is debated.'
(*The Evening Times*, 16 October 2002)

Reports about the latest adoption issue appeared in the press just two days after I had finished the first draft of this book. When I saw the one above, it encouraged me to continue with the process of completing the book - come hell or high water. Some may suggest that hell will visit me first!

It is interesting that sexuality is one of the few issues that can unite people from very disparate and, to a large extent, incompatible faith communities. It is also interesting that the headline for the article above was, 'Fight on Gay Adoption' which shows how the press can manipulate its readers. What the government of the UK was proposing was not a bill to introduce 'gay adoption', but one which would allow unmarried and same-sex couples to adopt. Before the bill's ultimate acceptance in the House of Lords (where there had been several bitter debates on the issue), only married couples and single people were able legally to adopt children. The debate on this issue focused more on homosexual partnerships than on unmarried couples, but it was interesting nonetheless to see both groups considered together. Sadly, the usual kinds of media conversations, full of ugly and aggressive language, quickly took us from a healthy debate to a place where conversation was no longer possible.

In June 2003, the UK government announced a consultation process with the focus of extending legal protections and rights to same-sex couples in England and Wales. Jacqui Smith, Deputy Minister for Women and Equality said, "Thousands of people are in long-term, stable, same-sex relationships. These are ordinary couples, living their lives and planning their futures together. They are committed to each other in all areas of their joint lives - but their relationships are invisible in the eyes of the law. Same-sex couples often face a range of humiliating, distressing and unnecessary problems because of a lack of legal recognition.'

She goes on to say that, 'Civil Partnership registration would underline the inherent value of committed same-sex relationships. It would support stable families and show that we really value the diversity of the society we live in. It would open the way to respect, recognition and justice for those who have been denied it too long. This is not about being "PC" but about bringing law and practice into line with the reality of people's lives.'[1]

In Scotland in 2003, the Green Party introduced a Bill - the Civil Registered Partnerships (Scotland) Bill - that would provide for similar protections in Scotland. It was not supported by the Scottish Executive but it showed that suddenly politicians are thinking pink!

The response from faith communities has been clear and predictable. Quoted in *The Guardian* (7 December 2002), Colin Hart, director of the Christian Institute, said, 'If the special benefits of marriage are given to those in homosexual relationships, then marriage becomes devalued.' And so it goes on. In Scotland Mario Conti, the Archbishop of Glasgow, has called on Members of the Scottish Parliament who are Catholic to resist the legislation allowing legal protection for same sex couples, a move

[1] www.stonewall.org.uk

which has been enthusiastically endorsed by the Vatican but which has ruffled the feathers of legislators who need to assert their independence from the church.

Another sign of change is the appointment of Rowan Williams to the See of Canterbury, a move which has delighted those who would call themselves liberal in the Church of England and has enraged (in equal measure) those who would not. At a recent discussion group held at the Greenbelt Festival in Cheltenham, England, an enthusiastic parishioner was overheard thanking God for Dr Williams' appointment as it would 'restore her faith in the Church of England'. What a burden! But it is true that his appointment has allowed discussions to take place that need to be out in the open. The problem with issues of sexuality is that we talk about them only when we absolutely have to. The taboo relating to sexuality is still a powerful force in our society - something peculiarly British.

Not everyone has been happy with Dr Williams' appointment and the opening of the floodgates for all sorts of difficult issues to be aired and discussed. George Curry of the Church Society is quoted as having said, 'The Bible tells us same-sex relationships are always sinful and wrong - we cannot have our leaders endorsing immorality - [Dr Williams] must be disciplined.'[2] And to think at this point Rowan Williams hadn't even started the job. It is sad that the discussion of his appointment did not focus on his abilities, or his vast experience that made him fit for the job, but instead got stuck on one particular issue.

Since his appointment we have seen how the Church of England and the wider Anglican Communion has continued to struggle with the issue. Witness the fiasco surrounding the appointment of Canon Jeffrey John as Bishop of Reading in the UK, and his subsequent decision - following untenable pressure - to turn down the appointment; and the ordination of an openly gay Bishop in the Episcopal Church of America, Rev Canon Gene Robinson, where the process became very ugly: these are are all pointers of a community that is not at ease with itself.

In Scotland, the Moderator of the General Assembly, Right Rev Professor Iain Torrance announced that he was 'untroubled' at the prospect of openly gay ministers being ordained to serve within the Church of Scotland. His opinion caused great debate within Scottish ecclesiastical circles, little of which was helpful or constructive, and all of which must have looked confusing to the interested outsider.

It's important to emphasise at this point that while this book focuses a great deal on the experience of gay and lesbian people, it does not claim to be particularly a 'gay book'. The reason for this particular focus is that the experience of gay and lesbian people helps us understand why other people in the churches who are different in some way - single, separated or divorced, living together, celibate etc - often express a feeling of not being full members of the family. The other reason is because it is made easier by the hysterical ways in which the issue of homosexuality is discussed in the church and the wider media.

2 *www.bbc.co.uk/news* - Monday 28 October 2002

The United Kingdom prides itself as being at the forefront of innovation in many ways - for instance in terms of technology, service industries, education and so on - and yet we still struggle with how to relate to one another in terms of our sexualities; we struggle at times even to acknowledge that we have them. But in a country where there is debate within some circles over the propriety of a future king marrying the woman he loves, one can be forgiven for thinking that we have lost the plot!

This book has been written from within the context and understanding of a venerable Christian denomination. The Church of Scotland has been around for a long time. It is lumbered not so much with baggage, as with truckloads of tradition and misery-inducing ways of being. How can it, and institutions like it, engage in the new day and age in which we live? Does giving a moral lead mean that we have to say 'no' to everything we are uncomfortable with or that we believe contradicts our understanding of scripture and our own ideals? Do we stick our heads in the sand and live in denial? Or do we engage with the conversations that are taking place today (with or without us) in ways that nourish and enrich, having the confidence that we may have something positive to say about the human condition in the twenty-first century? The choice is ours. My fear is that at the moment we are not making very good choices and that we can do better. Much of what follows is about identifying our problems and trying to figure out ways of moving forward.

There will be some who will damn this book and its author for being too liberal. Before they do so they should know that I have, in faith terms, grown up within a Charismatic Evangelical context and tradition and that this context is the one in which I personally feel most comfortable and at ease. I reserve the right, however, to use the brain and opportunities God has given me to think for myself and speak about things as I see them. Others will damn the book because it does not go far enough. They may be right. It will go only as far as I can take it and, having spent a number of years looking at these issues, what follows is my personal contribution to the discussion.

I hope that readers who feel that their opinions are 'fixed and sorted' on these issues might find something in this book to help them revisit the discomfort of uncertainty. This is the crucible of faith, the touching place with God. For those who feel disenfran-chised by the church in particular and by Christianity in general, I hope they will see that there are people in this thing we call church who have a bigger world-view than the media often portray. There are churches and Christian people who will learn from, not condemn, those who live outside traditional understandings of marriage relationships. There is room for us all.

For those on the right and left wings of the churches who want to continue their favourite game of "sexuality ping pong", I say a 'plague on both your houses!' Leave the rest of us to have a proper, liberating and respectful conversation about these issues which are so fundamental to our understanding of who we are, how we identify ourselves, how we love and live and how we become more human.

chapter 1

It started

without a kiss

Recently I spent six hours talking with a young man who had a difficult story to tell. He had become a Christian at a large evangelistic event some 10 years ago, and at a time when he was struggling to find faith he was also struggling with his sexual identity.

He was - and is - gay.

His story was familiar to me but his case is more extreme than most. For a period of about six years, this young man has been subjected to a most cruel and vindictive programme of counselling. He has been told the Devil lives in him. People have tried to exorcise his 'demons'. He has been told he has been healed. He has been told he is resisting the will of God. He has been told he is a failure. The sad thing is that he already felt he had failed and in an act of self-punishment, he turned to the very organisation that would confirm his failure for him - the Christian Church.

This young man, now in his mid-twenties, has never had a relationship with another man. Has never kissed another man. He has been emotionally abused by the churches he has been part of. He tells of times when members of a particular church would phone him at home to let him know they were praying about his sexuality. He talks of services where he was called down to the front of the church for ministry and the laying on of hands.

And yet after all that he is still gay and he still believes in God. If ever I needed an example of a hero of the faith then he would be it. The church has thrown everything at him but he has stood firm and what is left is a deep suspicion of the church alongside a beautiful sense of the mystery and purposes of God.

Sadly, this young man's story is not unique. Many young people and adults I have lived alongside and worked with in the last 20 years can tell similar stories. The church is still hung up about sex. It is the last taboo for us. It is the one single issue that threatens to tear us apart. It is the last battle for the soul of a church that is increasingly out of touch with the world in which it exists. But it's not just being gay that that draws such intolerant or unhelpful responses as the following story makes clear.

Katy's story
I was in the process of splitting up with my husband after a marriage of some seven years. People nowadays think that divorce is an easy thing - well it isn't. I don't think anyone would willingly go through that, I certainly never want to again. My marriage was not good - although I married a so-called Christian it wasn't an equal or loving relationship and I was abused emotionally if not physically. Being a good evangelical I was fortunate enough to find great friends who prayed for me during this terrible time. I could call on them at any time of the day for help, and sometimes went round to their house for prayer.

A girl in my house group from church asked if she could have lunch with me - I agreed. During the lunch she told me in no uncertain terms that if the people who were praying with me were not certified members of the Institute of Counsellors (or some such body) I was risking instant dismissal at my place of work for seeing them

*during working hours. Changing the subject
abruptly she then suggested that I should rejoice
with her, as she'd just discovered she was
pregnant. Great - just what I needed. I went
straight back to my boss and told him
(incidentally, not a Christian) that the people who
were helping me were not officially equipped to do
so. That didn't bother him in the slightest - he
was happy for me to receive whatever help I
needed as he could see the torment I was in.
Shades of the Good Samaritan, eh?*

*This might not sound so terribly important as
it's read now. I can only say that I was left numb
by this totally useless, hurtful and inappropriate
advice. I hope I never, ever treat anyone in a
similar way. To any of the legalistically minded
out there I'd like to put this question: before you
are ready to dish out the condemnation, where are
you at 3am when someone in severe emotional
pain is crying out to God from their bed?*

This is the voice of a woman in her late thirties. What she has said shows us that any
discussion about sexuality must not be seen just as a 'youth issue', though it would be
convenient for us if we could think it were. We journey with our sexualities throughout
our lives and so we have to think about sexuality as a lifelong process. It's not just about
good and bad behaviour; it's about who we are and how we live. But more importantly
it's about how we value and respect one another. Essentially, it's about being human.

Where are we going?

. . . .

This book is neither an academic tome nor is it a theological discourse. The intention is
for a conversation between the author, and you, the reader. I hope the book will help
you reflect on your own experiences of your own sexuality. I hope it will challenge you
to think about the kinds of conversations the church needs to have if it is to engage
with the sexual ethic that exists today. Fundamentally, I hope it will comfort you if you
are one of the many who have had your faith tested by a church that has failed you and
that in some small way these words might help you find a way home. If not to church,
then to the God who made you as you are, who cannot remember your sins and whose
welcome is as open and wide and warm as it ever was.

When Jesus was with us he pointed to the crowds of self-righteous people and condemned them. He turned their world-views upside down by his associations with the poor, the sinful, the lost and the outcast. When an inner circle wanted to absorb him he would dance with those who lived in the outer circle and offer those bewildered religious bigots the chance to be free. Sadly, many of them could not accept that freedom. It was too much for them, and they stayed imprisoned by their bigotry and prejudice, by their unthinking and unswerving sense of their own rightness.

How familiar a situation in today's church. Indeed, Episcopalian priest and best-selling author Robert Capon has said this, 'The church, by and large, has had a poor record of encouraging freedom. She has spent so much time inculcating in us the fear of making mistakes that she has made us like ill-taught piano students: we play our songs, but we never really hear them because our main concern is not to make music but to avoid some mistake that will get us in trouble.' (Robert Capon 1982, p.148) Today, God is calling us to make music. For many of us this will be a terrifying thought because we will be afraid of how the church will react, so disempowered have we become.

In the UK the Christian church as a whole is not growing, although for a variety of reasons its evangelical and charismatic wings are. Mainstream denominations struggle to contemporise the teachings of Jesus and generally fail miserably. Such institutions are inherently conservative and increasingly are subject to the sway of a vocal and articulate evangelical minority which feels it has the moral and ethical voice of God.

This is not one voice crying in the wilderness. It *is* the wilderness. For the church of Jesus Christ is lost and needs to be found again. One of the ways that it will be saved is through its attitudes to people and sexuality. The church needs to be saved. It needs to be saved for its own sake but more importantly for the sake of those who have not heard the pure message of the gospel.

People who 'misbehave' sexually - whether that is by having sex before marriage or being gay or being divorced or masturbating or using pornography (and I have met people in the Christian church who have done all these things) - need a place to go. They need someone to tell them the story of Jesus in a way that is non-judgmental and open. The church we have now does not wish to do this and therein lies the reason for its decline and decay. Today's church is for the 'well-behaved': the married, the happily and contentedly single, the widowed. The church will be good to them. But if you have misbehaved? Will it be good for you?

Author of *The Message* Eugene Peterson writes, 'All the persons of faith I know are sinners, doubters, uneven performers. We are not secure because we are sure of ourselves but because we trust that God is sure of us' (Eugene Peterson 1980, p. 86).

I asked the young man I talked about at the beginning of this chapter to tell me the things about himself that he liked. He couldn't list any. He wanted to tell me the things he didn't like but I wouldn't let him. It seems to me that his experience of life and of the church had taught him to hate himself. Surely it was hard enough for him to grow up feeling different without having to be part of a church that would abuse its position and try to change his identity? When I told him that for me to hear that after all he had gone through he was still seeking the Lord was fantastic, I could tell he was pleased to hear it but reluctant at the same time.

I had a similar experience recently with a young woman who happens to be a lesbian. She had given up going to church a long time ago because she just knew that being different meant she wasn't welcome. She had become friends with some of the young people I work with and had gradually joined in with things they were doing, including summer missions. At a recent event organised by the Church of Scotland, during which issues of sexuality were discussed, she talked about her sexuality and was promptly told by another member of the group that she was destined for hell. When I saw her she was hanging on to her faith by her fingertips. Sometimes I feel the church is not worthy of such faith.

God is sure of the young man and the two women mentioned in this chapter. There are many in the church who will never be sure of them just because they are gay or divorced or unmarried. This book is not an attempt to change anyone's mind. It is not a theological rant against a regime that hurts and abuses people. Instead it is a vocabulary book that might help people from all parts of the church and none to begin to discuss issues of sexuality in new, vibrant and useful ways. If we don't develop this vocabulary, if we don't begin to have more useful conversations about sexuality, then people like those mentioned here will pay the price. Young people in particular may be more likely to look for support in places which may not be good for them. Older people may feel simply abandoned and so may fade into the shadows. If people cannot find what they need in the church then they may be compelled to find it elsewhere. Do we care?

Jesus says, 'Follow me'. He didn't say where. He didn't say with whom. He didn't tell us we'd get to pick the team. People who are deemed to misbehave sexually today are treated like the last ones to be picked for a game on a school play-ground. If you are one of these, be reassured that in the Kingdom of God, the last shall be first (Matthew 19:30).

chapter 2

Moral panic!

On Friday 14 June 2002, the world almost stopped spinning on its axis. The headlines on front pages of the newspapers that day focused on new research that suggested that 'sex education has little effect on teenage lifestyles'. Worse was to come when it was also suggested through the same research that sex education had 'little effect on teen pregnancies'. Later that month, Jack McConnell, the First Minister of Scotland, hit the headlines when he stepped in to stop Lothian Health Board's plan to make the morning-after pill available to young women in the secondary schools in the Board's area. He was apparently applauded by teacher's groups, parent's groups and (surprise!) religious groups for taking such a tough stance.

Does this mean anything beyond the rhetoric that accompanies such headlines? What are the real issues? It's clear they are important and it's right that we should be concerned; but are we brave enough to ask difficult questions of ourselves and face the consequences our answers may bring?

Sex education in schools

When I was a teacher I was often aware that when things seemed to go wrong with young people in society, the response was generally, 'What are the teachers doing?' It is clear that in terms of young people learning about sex, teachers are doing a great deal. Some very positive programmes are being run in schools throughout the UK, but we have to move on from the naïve assumption that because such education is on offer, everyone is actually learning.

Formal sex education in schools is only one way for young people to learn. We need to evaluate our aims and objectives for such programmes and the resources that we use in them continually to ensure that they suit the experience and aspirations of young people in the twenty-first century. In many cases, people who are delivering the programmes have world-views - both moral and ethical - which are unlikely to match those of their pupils.

I went through puberty in the 1970s. That's a long time ago. The context in which young women and men experience puberty today has changed significantly. Sex is a commercial product. It has long since left the arena of the bedroom and is now regarded as a commodity active in virtually every consumer product. Sex is everywhere and therefore formal sex education programmes - whatever their worth - have to compete with forces possibly much more potent and visible and engaging with the target audience. This point is affirmed by social scientists Epstein and Johnston who state, 'The contemporary accentuation of sexual identities owes much to the salience of the sexual in the advertisement, retailing and consumption of commodities of all kinds' (Epstein and Johnson 1998, p. 41).

Today, when a commercial organisation chooses to use a sexual image to promote a product it does so with a degree of knowledge about its customers. Not all sex education programmes are drawn up with such attention to detail; many still operate on the assumption that the adult generation has 'the truth' if only the youngsters would listen!

Simon Forest, head of the Sex Education Forum in the UK, suggests that we shouldn't even expect teachers to change the behaviour of teenagers, that this can happen only in partnership with other agencies and individuals. 'When you deliver a lesson in the classroom to 13 year olds, some are pre-pubescent, some may be going out with someone, some are in the throes of puberty and some might have had sex: that's a hard group to target. We need more information in the community so that young people can select it themselves' (*The Guardian*, 14 February 2002).

What this means is that parents need to be involved. Local youth clubs, health centres, libraries, internet services and churches also need to see themselves as providers of sex education and to find ways of doing that well in ways which are relevant to young people's lives.

The political agenda

Unfortunately the discussion around sex education has become too heavily politicised. Many politicians and large sections of the media do not actually help this situation - they prefer to turn up the heat. If we take the example of the morning-after pill (see above), Mr McConnell may have been politically astute - the young people in question have no power to vote anyone out of office, and those who do may have fairly conventional ideas about this particular form of contraception. The hypocrisy which lies at the heart of this debate - if it is a debate at all - is in the fact that we say we want young people to make responsible choices about their sexualities and sexual practices and yet we do not want to face up to the consequences of those choices. If we expect young people to be responsible that means we have to give them the tools - not just the information - to help them to do that. While many of us may find the provision of the morning-after pill in a secondary school morally dubious, it may be the lesser evil in preventing another teenage pregnancy, with all that that means. This is a difficult choice for us today, but one we must not shirk.

The wider context

Young people's attitudes to and experience of sex will be formed within a wide web of relationships. Parents, friends, other family members, the media and so on all have a part to play, as does the culture of the community in which they live. Poverty levels and levels of employment and unemployment, levels of educational attainment - all these things can affect how a young person will understand and work out her or his sexuality.

A young person growing up in an urban priority area may well have a different experience of sex education from one growing up in a prosperous suburb. For any young person (or indeed, anyone at all), sex with a partner may be simply a form of recreation. It may not be about affirming a relationship in the way that other people might understand this. Instead it might just be something that seems appropriate to the moment; something that may or may not be repeated. Ultimately, for the participants at least, it may be something that has no moral or ethical dimension to it at all. It can be simply something to do that seems nice. We might be shocked by this but it may be true that sex for many young people has to be understood in recreational terms as well as those in which it has been traditionally understood.

Relationship education

The Department of Health has suggested that 'international research shows that countries such as the Netherlands that have good sex and relationship education and high quality contraceptive advice services for young people have the lowest teenage conception rates.' It seems that there is a useful lesson here in terms of how we plan for the future. The first thing is that sex education needs to be firmly set into the context of relationships. It needs to be more organic and not just about biology and mechanics. Human beings have an innate ability to find out what goes where - what we need help with is to understand how we relate to other people in sexual ways.

This has been borne out by the government's own schools watchdog, Ofsted. In its report, *Sex and Relationships*, it is suggested that most schools are 'conscientious' in terms of their teaching about sex and relationships but that only the basic facts of life are being taught well. There is a lack of emphasis on how we make and sustain relationships, how we approach parenthood and how we avoid infection. Perhaps we need to re-brand sex education altogether. We need education programmes which take account of the kinds of relationship that young people have today and which they may wish to have in the future. How do we help young people make good choices in the situations that face them now and, in developmental terms, how do we assist them to become what they would like to become?

There is no easy answer here except to say that this can never be the full responsibility of teachers or schools. We all need to play our part. And there is no hiding place for the churches. We have to engage our minds and hearts with these issues and start the conversations where young people are, rather than trying to provide answers to questions they aren't even asking.

Young people need services that will give them information and advice they need at the times they need it. When I go out dancing (something I have discovered in mid-life!) and go to the loo I am confronted by a box of free condoms together with a note that encourages me to have safe sex. The owners of the club are working with health agencies and are helping their customers to make responsible choices. What might such reasoned and responsible choices be for young people?

It is obvious that such information and services need to be available where young people are. We still have a culture that expects young people to come to us or to go to a particular facility when they want information about sex. Instead, sexual health clinics and other services should be freely available in places where young people can access the services without necessarily having to ask an adult if it's okay to go there. That doesn't mean that the services won't be provided by adults, simply that we make it easier for young people to use those services. And yes, it is important - particularly if we want our young men to see contraception as their responsibility too - that condoms are freely available in school lavatories.

Some people will feel that simply having the condoms there will encourage young people to go out and have sex. Latest evidence would seem to contradict this. Young people are having sex, getting infected and having kids too young, whether or not they receive sex education. This may mean that the "morning-after" pill needs to be available in our schools, too. At least this would mean that young people would then have the opportunity to discuss their situation with a school nurse and possibly a guidance teacher. This is not only good practice but it is also about showing young people respect, helping them to see the consequences of their actions and perhaps learning from them. In these discussions we need to try to avoid extremes - so often the tool used by political agitators - so that we can find some ground where we can talk about this type of situation clearly. Making services and information more freely available is not the symbol of a society that is suffering from moral collapse. Rather, it is a symbol of a society that places trust and respect in professionals who work with young people and in the young people themselves. The UK government has said it wants to cut the number of teenage pregnancies significantly in the medium term and is currently trialling the provision of the "morning after" pill in schools in a number of areas. In one such area, Nottingham, where the teenage pregnancy rate is double the national average, organisations opposed to this initiative fear that young women will be pressured into having sex more often - we will have to wait and see. But unless we take some difficult decisions like this, it is unlikely that the aim of reducing teenage pregnancy will be achieved, and many more young women in the UK will have children before they are ready for them. This kind of complex moral situation cannot have any single answer that won't throw up other moral dilemmas. What we have to do is to try to make the best provision possible for the people who need it most and then try to help them make the best possible choices.

Services for young people

Health boards, GP surgeries and other health-related organisations need to consider how best to make appropriate services available to the young people in their communities. It may be that positive partnerships can be developed between such agencies, youth workers and young people in the community so that the services provided are used.

'In the 1970s the UK had a similar teenage birth rate to other European states but by the late 1990s it was twice as high as Germany, three times as high as France and six times as high as the Netherlands' (*The Guardian*, 29 June 2002). How much more evidence do we need before we will make better choices on behalf of our young people and more importantly *with* them? Young people need to be involved in discussions about the provision and delivery of appropriate services. Moral panic serves only the self-righteous. It does not provide solutions. Instead, it uses young people as a battleground for ideology and political rhetoric that is more about wielding and gaining power than it is about fairness or justice or understanding.

In the area of Scotland round Glasgow - where some women in the poorest parts of the city become grandmothers at around the same age women in the more affluent areas are considering having their first child - the decision has been made to appoint a teenage pregnancy 'czar'. Following similar, apparently successful, initiatives in England, this new post will have the responsibility of reducing the alarmingly high teenage pregnancy rates in the city, where one in ten first-time mothers are under the age of 16. In 2000, 9464 teenagers became pregnant in Scotland and 4000 went on to terminate those pregnancies.[1] This chilling statistic is one that is not going to go away just by showering it with moral indignation or simplistic answers. Services for young people need to fit the world in which they live.

Gay and lesbian young people

In early 2000, Donald Dewar, First Minister of Scotland, announced the intention of the Scottish Executive to repeal Section 28 of the Local Government Act 1988 on the grounds that it discriminated against homosexuals. Section 28, or Clause 2a as it was known in Scotland, had been introduced by the previous Conservative administration in the UK. It sought to prevent local authorities from intentionally "promoting homosexuality" or publishing any material that had the same intention. Authorities were also forbidden to promote homosexuality in schools as an acceptable or "pretended" family relationship.

At the height of the debate that followed in Scotland, many voices clamoured for attention. They all hoped that their words would make headlines. Within that clamour there were very few young people's voices. This is understandable. How many gay or lesbian young people would have the courage to stand up in that kind of atmosphere and talk about themselves?

[1] *The Scotsman*, 13 August 2003; 'Bid to cut teen pregnancies', Kizzy Taylor

Thankfully some did. Moray Paterson, a former pupil of Portobello High School in Edinburgh, described in The Scotsman newspaper his experience of being a young, gay man at school, and in particular, how the sex education offered by the school had little or no relevance for him. When he was at school he kept quiet about his sexuality. He had seen what had happened to an openly gay fellow-student at the hands of bullies and so he felt he was forced to live a 'double life'. He was afraid to come out or be open about his sexuality for fear that something as bad, or worse, would happen to him.

Paterson felt particularly excluded during sex education lessons because the basic assumption of all that he was taught was that everyone in the class was heterosexual. He talks of the missed opportunity - of how much better he would have felt about himself if there had been advice on offer relevant to his life. His own sex education came when he began to visit a local gay club. 'Section 28 prevented me getting a proper sexual education and that devalues your existence', he said.

This surely cannot be right. When we provide sex education for a group of young people we cannot assume we are working with a homogenous group. If we do, we run the risk some of the group will not only made to feel left out but devalued and their very existence called into question. We also fail such young people in that they leave school ill-equipped for their sexual lives. Politically, it may be that this is the acceptable "collateral damage" in the ideological war that rages in political and religious circles about these issues. What does it really matter if gay and lesbian young people are left without the proper information and skills required to make positive choices about their sexualities? What does it really matter if they end up being hurt or infected with sexually transmitted infections (STIs)? Are young people at risk of contracting HIV because we don't have the courage to give them the information they need?

If we are to make progress, any sex and relationship education programmes running in our schools must be supported by properly funded and resourced initiatives in the local community. And they must understand their users. They need to recognise that some of the young people involved will be gay. These young people will not necessarily need advice about getting pregnant or on the basic biology and mechanics of heterosexual intercourse. They will need information and advice appropriate to them and their situations. They will need places where they can discuss their own issues and see that these issues are given the same weight and respect as those of their heterosexual colleagues. This is not utopian - it is common sense.

However, only recently it was said that in the opinion of one researcher, 'Gay and lesbian young people are "unknown creatures" in adolescent research, in youth policy and in planning of help for young people as well as social work with adolescents. Little attention is paid to the "silent side" of growing up, to the struggle to find one's place in a rigidly heterosexual and sexually polarised order.' (S Hark, 2000)

These words are contained in research carried out by Mike Breitbart in Germany. The research has identified that the lack of positive role models for gay and lesbian young people is a key issue. In Germany, the government funds a voluntary organisation (SCHLau, or 'Schwul-lesbisches Aufklärung') which arranges for gay and lesbian adults to visit schools to discuss being homosexual with young people. In his research, Mike talks about how this type of process has developed in Sweden (since the early 1970s) and how it began in Germany in the early 1980s. So these issues seem to be discussed in much more open and mature ways by some of our European neighbours. Perhaps a more positive discussion about sexuality in schools may not be impossible to achieve - even if we are perhaps decades behind other countries in this. It is indeed encouraging to hear of the work being developed by the organisation LGBT Youth Scotland, which is beginning to make connections with young people and youth work organisations in the greater Edinburgh area.

This isn't about being politically correct, it's about issues of honesty and justice. Mike Breitbart's research shows that having a more explicit approach to homosexuality in school-based sex education programmes may achieve the following outcomes:

- The event (i.e. visit of the gay or lesbian youth worker/educator) leads to a positive change in attitudes of the young people who take part towards gay and lesbian young people.

- For some young people this event provides an opportunity to ask questions and deal with important issues.

- These opportunities can lead to changed behaviour and increased respect for gay and lesbian young people.

(Breitbart M, 2001)

In May 2003 a book was published in which the authors called for a more open and honest approach to be adopted in sex education in British schools including emphasis on homosexuality. Professor Michael Reiss, one of the authors, said that homosexuality should be taught in schools by specially trained and willing teachers 'partly out of respect for those pupils who are gay, and partly to prepare all pupils for today's world in which sexual orientation issues are never out of the news.'[2] If education is about liberation, then such an approach is worthy of consideration. Our understanding of how we educate the young about sex and relationships needs to be liberated from an ethos that runs in direct contradiction to what young people actually do and want. In Scotland, and perhaps throughout the UK, if such an initiative were introduced there would probably be an outcry and the usual suspects would get onto their warhorses and fight the good fight. Many of these people seem to think that homosexuality is a virus that can be caught like the 'flu - and perhaps avoided like it.

In 1988 Lord Halsbury introduced a Bill into the House of Lords, a precursor to Section 28 (Clause 2a), in which he made a distinction between 'acceptable' and

[2] www.bbc.news.co.uk: 'Call for sex education update', 29 May 2003

'unacceptable' homosexuality. According to Epstein and Johnson, Halsbury defined the 'unacceptable' homosexual to be one who suffered from a 'psychological syndrome' the key features of which were exhibitionism, proselytising and boasting of homosexual achievements (Epstein and Johnson 1998, p. 41). Would there be a similar response if we agreed to bring homosexuality out of the closet in our schools and allow gay and lesbian educators to visit schools and talk about being gay?

We have to take responsible approaches - all stakeholders need to take their responsibilities seriously. We can no longer avoid these issues. Navigating the sexual seas is not easy for any of us. We have to recognise that sex is a commodity that is being sold to young people every day of their lives. They need to hear reasoned and helpful voices which convey an understanding of complex issues and which offer non-judgmental, useful advice and appropriate sexual health services. Such services need to be inclusive. They need to appreciate diversity and see such educational programmes as opportunities for all of us to come out of the closet, recognising that there are people among us who sleep with people of the same gender, and that they have the same rights as everyone does to good advice and appropriate services.

Thank heavens for organisations in Scotland like HEBS (Health Education Board for Scotland), and Healthy Respect. Both have websites which provide positive resources that deal with such issues. The Healthy Respect site is especially valuable because it is designed specifically with and for young people. Young people can go to this site to ask questions they might be afraid to ask anywhere else, and they will get positive information and encouragement that will help them to make better choices.

Another example of a positive development in this area is The Place in Glasgow which provides a full range of sexual health services for young people. This is an imaginative collaboration between local authority, health board and community education services. Workers from a variety of professions provide an informal and relaxed environment in which young people can discuss their questions and problems and receive guidance as appropriate. The people involved in these projects are the prophets of our age and point to how things are going to have to be if we are to ensure a just and safe sexuality education and health programme for our young people.

But the churches need to get involved too. We have hesitated on the margins of this discussion for too long. If we care about people, if we have any real understanding of what salvation actually means, then we will not be content until we are in the very middle of these issues engaging with young people and professionals alike. We must be the ones who are asking questions and learning ourselves, as well as advising and trying to restore the moral and ethical dimension to sex and sexuality which pervasive secularism, materialism and individualism have taken away.

This is no mean feat. But if we don't attempt it then we lose the right to be even a voice in the wilderness. We will not have a voice. We will remain in a barren land, talking to ourselves.

chapter 3

Here

and now

We live in constant sexual revolution.
We always have. It is a myth to think
that there was ever a time when
sexual understanding or practice was
unchanging. We might like to think,
like the poet Philip Larkin, that in the
UK we only discovered sex in the
1960s, but in reality it has always been
hard to ignore - a design fault perhaps!

There are two golden rules for
this discussion. One is to resist the
temptation to believe that there was
ever a golden age when everyone
behaved well and did the right thing;
the other is to realise that all we can
deal with is the way people live now.
We need to try to learn as much as
we can about that, so that we can
respond in appropriate ways and join
people on their journeys.

The key issues today

. . . .

The key issues for today are:

- The 'collapse' of the nuclear family
- The growth of gay and lesbian identity
- The sexuality of older people
- A new openness about child sexual abuse
- A new openness about domestic violence
- Increasing incidence of sexually transmitted infections (STIs)
- The continuing and global HIV/AIDS pandemic
- Teenage pregnancy

We will look at each of these issues in turn because they provide the basis for this vocabulary book. We need to know about behaviour patterns and to try to understand them, and then we need to think about how to respond.

When I say 'we', I don't mean to suggest that this book is written by someone who has everything sorted out, or that it is intended for those who consider themselves to be so. At this point I am very conscious of the words of Henri Nouwen, 'He who thinks he is finished, is finished. How true. Those who think that they have arrived, have lost their way. Those who think they have reached their goal, have missed it. Those who think they are saints, are demons.'[1]

There is such a danger in being stuck, in feeling that we have arrived at a point that demands no more movement from us. There is an air of 'stuck-ness' about the church and its views on sexuality. The church would do well to listen to Nouwen's words.

Any understanding we gain will benefit ourselves before anyone else. This is not a textbook, it's a mirror. We need to look into it, think about what we are seeing and then do something about it. And when we see someone else's reflection, instead of getting angry with them, we should remember our own image, keep quiet, and begin a journey with that person which will lead to our own salvation.

The 'collapse' of the nuclear family

. . . .

The word 'collapse' is used deliberately. It is intended to be emotive. How does it make you feel? What do you think about the way family life is working out today? What are the reasons for any changes you see? What is the church doing to help? What can it do?

For me the word 'family' is a dangerous and deadly one. I grew up in what is now

---

[1] Henri Nouwen, as quoted in Mike Yaconnelli 2001, page 16

called a single-parent family. My mother and father separated when I was two years old. This was in the 1960s and it was a less usual situation to be in then - something I was always aware of. Some of us might make all sorts of assumptions about how the child of such parents would be likely to turn out; single-parent families have had a bad press. There is in fact no such thing as a single-parent family. I was 'parented' by many more people than just my mother. The Africans have a lovely phrase for this, used by Hilary Rodham Clinton in the title of one of her books: they say that 'it takes a village to raise a child'. They're right: I was raised by a village, something I will always be thankful for.

I tell my story here not to deny the obvious difficulties that living in non-traditional families can produce, but to show that living in such families is not necessarily a cause for concern. There were times when my 'village' did very well and times where it let me down badly. The same is true for every child. The point of this is to highlight the need for the 'village' to reflect on its role in current trends in family life.

Marriage is not as popular as it used to be. The government's own agency for statistics, the Office for National Statistics (ONS), has gathered some key indicators which show the major changes in family life over the last 50 years. These are:

❖ the number of marriages has dropped by a quarter

❖ the annual number of divorces has seen a five-fold increase

❖ four in ten marriages today are remarriages for one or both partners - twice the comparable rate in 1952

❖ living together (cohabitation) is now the most common form of first partnership

❖ 40% of babies are now born outside marriage

❖ 20% of children live in one-parent families.[2]

Hilary Rodham Clinton says, 'You can't roll up your sleeves and get to work if you're still wringing your hands' (1996, p. 17). And that's precisely what the church needs to do today. We need to stop wringing our hands, or pointing our fingers, about the way family life is evolving.

It is true that divorce and remarriage cause families dreadful problems and concerns - sometimes fatal ones in terms of 'normal' family life. But they do not necessarily cause family life as we know or understand it to disappear. Increasing divorce rates, while problematic, have positive aspects to them in that people are no longer willing to stay in loveless, faithless or violent marriages - which can only be a good thing, especially if children are involved. And people living together without being married need not represent the collapse of civilisation as we know it. It is hardly surprising that more people are choosing to live together and not marry. Most children are still being brought up within a two-parent family unit. So when I used the term 'collapse' earlier, I

[2] *Fifty Years of Change*, Office for National Statistics, UK 2002

was perhaps being over-dramatic. The family is alive and well in ways that we understand; but what has changed, I think, is the 'village' which surrounds it.

When I was a child, I spent much time being cared for by my grandmother. My mother had to go out to work - single parents had no other options then - and so I spent many of my early days with my grandmother. Sometimes she was more like my mother than my mum, because she was older and seemed less chaotic and more reliable. As well as my grandmother, my grandfather and my mum's siblings were all involved in my care. They were all around and part of my everyday life. Then there was the wider 'village' - neighbours and friends of the family who were part of the intricate web of life surrounding and protecting me and the other children within it.

It is the village that is in danger of collapse, I think, not the family. This has put a great strain on the family and is one of the reasons why divorce is so high in this and other countries. We don't necessarily look out for each other within the wider 'village' any more. We are often separated even from our immediate families - by geography, by pace of life, by work.

The church and the 'village'...................

The churches have opportunities to provide 'village' experiences for families today, and they should do so for any kind of family - not just the ones that they approve of. Many churches offer after-school clubs, homework clubs, parent and toddler groups and nursery care. This is a key area of mission for the church. I once visited a congregation in the West End of Glasgow and there I found elderly women bemoaning the fact that on Sundays mothers would bring their kids and drop them off at the Sunday School and then would nip over to the supermarket to do the family shopping! The members of that congregation felt they were being used by these women, instead of celebrating the opportunity represented by this development.

The church has lots of opportunities to support family life today. Are we ready to stop pointing our fingers or wringing our hands and roll up our sleeves, think and act - or do we prefer to live under the myth of the 'collapse' of family life?

The growth of gay and lesbian identity.......

Openness about sexuality - particularly gay sexuality - is a very recent thing and we should bear that in mind at all times. When we look into history we see that homosexuality has been interpreted in very different ways in different cultures and societies. There has never been a universal view that it is 'good' or 'bad'.

Because of this recent opening up, it sometimes seems as though homosexuality has just been discovered in the UK. Gay and lesbian people are everywhere you look. From soap operas on television, to television and film personalities and politicians, our world is gradually going pink! One could be forgiven for thinking that Britain is becoming a much more liberal and tolerant society.

Historically, tolerance towards homosexuality is a very recent phenomenon in the UK. Anal sex was made illegal during the reign of Henry VIII and the law remained static until the late 1800s when Henry Labouchere, a Liberal MP, proposed that any type of sex between two men be considered criminal. Thus punishment was extended to any act of 'gross indency'. Lesbianism was never incorporated into law - when the issue of sex between women was raised in Parliament, the peer in question was 'told to shut up on the grounds that he would only advertise its existence to an impressionable public'.[3] All this took place at a time when girls of around 13 years old could be bought as sex slaves in London. The scandal which followed the exposure of this trade resulted in the legal age of consent for women being raised from 13 to 16 years.

Today there are some signs of a new tolerance towards homosexuality - the Scottish Parliament's repeal of Section 28/ Clause 2a and the UK government's recent decisions to extend a variety of rights to gay and lesbian people are key indicators of a society which is more at ease with gay and lesbian issues than in previous generations.

According to the Scottish Social Attitudes 2000 survey, published by the National Centre for Social Research, gay and lesbian lifestyles are becoming more socially acceptable. The survey offered a comparison between attitudes expressed in 2000 and those expressed on the same issues in 1983. Specifically relating to homosexuality, the survey showed that in 1983, sixty per cent of the people surveyed in Scotland thought that it was 'always wrong'. In 2000, the figure had dropped to 38%.[4] In 2001, an opinion poll for BBC television's *Panorama* programme suggested that 61% of those polled were in favour of same-sex couples being able to register their partnerships and 74% believed that the same rights should be extended to heterosexual co-habiting couples.[5]

However while some people will be happy with these developments, for others there is still a long way to go. The Terrence Higgins Trust, which campaigns on issues relating to HIV/AIDS, suggests that homophobia (prejudice or discrimination against lesbians and gay men) is still deeply rooted in British society. The Trust offers the following observations:

❖ Homophobia is widespread in society and has an effect on everyone.

❖ The British are less homophobic than Americans but more homophobic than the Germans and the Swedish.

❖ Women are less homophobic than men.

[3] Alan Travis, 'Repercussions of Scandals still Linger': *The Guardian*, 20 November 2002

[4] Hamish MacDonnell and David Scott, *The Scotsman*, 27 July 2001

[5] As reported in *The Guardian*, 7 December 2002

❖ Older people are likely to be more homophobic than younger people.

❖ Educated people are likely to be less homophobic than the lesser educated.

(The Terrence Higgins Trust, *Autumn Newsletter* 1999)

A report also recently published by the Trust in conjunction with Stonewall, another campaigning organisation, showed the results of a survey of 307 schools in England in 1998. It found that 80% of schools were aware of cases of 'verbal homophobic abuse'. A quarter of the schools reported physical attacks on pupils who were gay - or *assumed* to be gay. The survey also found that although nearly all schools had a policy on bullying, only 6% of the schools made explicit reference to homophobic-inspired bullying in their policies.

More recent reports confirm these findings and go on to suggest that up to 40% of young lesbian, gay or bisexual people have attempted suicide because they have been bullied at school. This research was carried out by MESMAC ('men who have sex with men, action in the community') Newcastle in conjunction with the College of York St John and Teeside University. Although the number of people in the study was small, enough evidence came through to suggest that gay and lesbian young people were facing severe difficulties in terms of bullying at school. Unfortunately, in England and Wales Section 28 is still in force, which means that teachers may be afraid to take direct action to stamp out homophobic bullying in case they are accused of promoting homosexuality.

It is interesting that when steps are taken to deal with issues such as bullying in schools, the people who are most often against such initiatives are people from the more conservative wings of the churches. When the General Teaching Council for Wales proposed drawing up a code of conduct designed to respect the rights and needs of homosexuals, the Christian Institute responded by opposing the section relating to gay and lesbian young people. Indeed, the Institute has opposed most of the advances mentioned in this section.

While respecting the views of those who have concerns about gay and lesbian people having more rights, visibility and acceptance in general, in the case of homophobic bullying in schools one wonders what these people might offer as solutions to the problem. One also wonders if they feel any sense of responsibility, in that their pronouncements, and the way they are reported in the media, do not help to resolve such problems but rather provide ammunition for those who might wish to exacerbate them.

It is clear that even though some of us may be comfortable with an increased visibility of gay and lesbian issues, that does not mean that gay, lesbian, bisexual or transgendered people in our communities will be immune from bigotry, hatred or prejudice.

So we in the church are faced with a dilemma. For a variety of reasons, some people are not comfortable with the increased visibility of gay and lesbian people. On the other hand, are we not meant to stand up to those who want to oppress gay - or indeed any other - people? Sadly, the church is often the place where oppressive attitudes are bred, and this will be discussed in more detail later.

What does the church have to offer gay and lesbian people? What do we have to offer each other in understanding our own sexualities and not being afraid to admit that we all find people of the same gender attractive in a variety of ways? This does not mean we want to sleep with them but that we are allowed to appreciate people of our own gender.

J L Empereur, a Jesuit priest, suggests that 'God has chosen some to be gay or lesbian as a way of revealing something of himself that heterosexuals do not' (Empereur 1998). How are we to react to that? It is a remarkable statement for a churchman to make.

Regardless of our theological positions about homosexuality or our experience of gay and lesbian people, such people *are* much more visible than they used to be, and attitudes towards them are becoming more tolerant. What is the right position for the church to take on this issue? What words do we need to add to our vocabulary to allow us to make a more useful contribution to the debate?

The sexuality of older people

There is a myth in our society that older people stop having sex. This is complete nonsense! People are living longer now and having sex well into old age. This presents a peculiar problem for us because it seems we are quite uncomfortable with the idea of our parents and grandparents continuing to enjoy sex. We prefer the idea of them being gentle, sexless beings who exist primarily to support the rest of us and give us a sense of history!

One of the issues was highlighted for me recently when I read a problem page in a national newspaper. The letter writer was in his late 60s and was going out with a woman of similar age who was insisting that they used a condom when they had sex. The man wasn't too keen on doing so, believing that now they were older 'everything would be okay'.

Myth number one - older people don't have sex. Wrong! Myth number two - older people always know how to have safe sex. Wrong again! Many older people are getting together, for whatever reason - perhaps because of the death, divorce or separation from spouse or partner. They are far from accepting that their sex lives are over! This points to another gap in the vocabulary. Older people need sex advice and education - not least because things have changed a lot since they may have had their first sexual encounter. We might note that in 1999 the BBC in England ran a series of programmes that gave safe sex advice specifically for older people. Using a variety of mature celebrities, the programmes covered all aspects of sexuality and offered back-up information which people could send away for.

According to Mary Gilhooley of the British Society of Gerontology, 'The sexual desire and expression of older people is often neglected. We have taken up the challenge to rectify the stereotyping and discrimination of older people. Our task is to make sure that older people are seen in all their diversity and not diminished by the narrow and harmful stereotypes which persist in our society. This has implications for us all, whatever our age.'[6]

And let's not forget the health benefits. Professor Ian Philp, the so-called 'old-age tsar' has said that, 'Sexually active older people live longer and stay healthier than their celibate counterparts. Sex can help elderly people stay healthy like any exercise, yet it seems that the sexual interest remains particularly strong in elderly women.'[7] Slowly, the sexuality of older people is coming out of the closet. It seems unlikely that the 'baby boomer' generation, now moving into its sixties, will stop wanting to have sex so this is an issue that perhaps become more openly discussed in the next few years.

The churches in the West are full of older people - many of whom might need such advice. Will it be made available to them, and will the churches be involved in this conversation, or will we prefer to live under the illusions of 'no sex please - we're older'? Any new vocabulary we develop about sex and sexuality must include the needs and issues specific to older people.

A new openness about child sexual abuse . . . . .

It has been a recent feature of my work that increasing numbers of young people - especially young women - are finding a voice and a place to talk about having been sexually abused at some point in their lives. There are few words that can be properly used to describe this tragedy or to help the lives that have been irrevocably changed as a result of the sins of others. It is clear that if we are developing a vocabulary that will nourish conversations about sexuality then we need to include this topic in that vocabulary. If we do not, then many young people will remain imprisoned by a past which will have a detrimental affect upon them for the rest of their lives.

According to organisations like Survivors Swindon, (*www.survivorswindon.com*) the current estimates about the prevalence of child sex abuse suggest that 1 in 4 males and 1 in 3 females will have experienced some form of sexual abuse before reaching the age

[6] BBC News, 12 September 2002

[7] BBC News, 13 September 2001

page 30

of 18. These are staggering numbers and yet we are only just beginning to let survivors talk about what has happened to them. Often they don't want to talk, because they feel nobody will believe them. Often they feel that they must have been to blame for what happened. Often they are left with a sense of being 'dirty', a feeling that cannot be dislodged and which haunts them in otherwise happy moments.

Only now are the churches in the West really waking up to this issue; and in doing so they have placed more emphasis on the aspect of self-protection than in providing safe places for survivors to talk about what has happened to them. It is understandable that institutions will want to defend themselves against being involved with such occurrences, but it is also important that we put as much effort into finding ways to bring healing to people in our churches and beyond who need it. Again this can be helped by all of us beginning to talk about the situation. As we will see later in this book, once a situation is discussed openly it allows those who might otherwise have said nothing to find their voice and speak, and this is how the healing can begin.

A new openness about Domestic Violence

There is another key area that needs to inform the development of this new vocabulary. A survey carried out by the BBC in early 2003 suggested that 1 in 4 adults had experienced some form of domestic violence. The survey had covered people in all forms of relationships, both long and short term. The survey suggested that more women experienced domestic violence than men and that they were more likely to report it to the police than men. More worrying still are the findings that suggest that many people believe there are circumstances in which violence is justified: e.g. if a partner has been unfaithful, or if a partner nags particularly badly.

While it is important to bear in mind that this is a phenomenon that is common to both genders, it is obvious that the majority of victims of it will be women. There is still much to be done in the discourse between the genders about women being equal and the need for men to view them as such. There are still aspects of this discourse that seem to imply that women are still somehow the possessions of their menfolk. The church needs to be a place where all victims of domestic abuse can be open about this and can hope to be believed. What happens, for instance, if the minister's spouse is being abused? Where do they turn to? This problem has been highlighted in a recent article in the Church of Scotland's own magazine, *Life and Work* (February 2003), and needs to be talked about more openly and honestly. Part of our problem might be a reluctance to live in the real world where these things happen, and there can be a mistaken assumption, just because we *are* the church, that they can't happen here. If we want to develop an honest vocabulary about sexuality then we need to think about the words that we use and the space that we offer, which might help women and men who suffer at the hands of their partners to find a road to healing and wholeness.

So here's the big picture. People are still getting married but many of them get divorced. The nuclear family is being replaced by the blended family. More people are choosing to be single. Gay and lesbian people are becoming more visible and their lifestyles are gaining more acceptance as part of mainstream life. Sex is no longer the sole prerogative of the young. People are being abused as children and by their partners.

This is sexuality as we experience it today. Sex is about life. Life is about sex. Death is the only sexless and lifeless state. Is the church on the side of life or death?

chapter 4

Bad boys and girls?

In the last chapter we looked at the bigger picture, the sexual map that defines the landscape of the UK. In this chapter we will look at two key behavioural issues - the incidence of Sexually Transmitted Infections (STIs) and teenage pregnancy. Both are symptoms of a dysfunctional society, reluctant to be grown up and to accept its responsibilities to care for people who are vulnerable. Both are symptoms of a lack of care and respect for one another. And each issue represents a huge area of learning for the church in terms of acquiring the vocabulary to address it, and also in terms of responding with compassion and appropriate action.

Increasing incidence of sexually transmitted infections (STIs)

I was told the 'facts of life' when I was aged 12 in a first-year science class at school. When I told my mother that I had learned the 'facts of life' her only comment was that she hoped I'd been listening! We never discussed them again. Well, I did listen (to some of it at least), and one aspect that I found fascinating and frightening was references made to a 'special clinic' where people could go if they found themselves to be in possession of some unfortunate disease after taking part in illicit sexual activity. I was terrified that I might ever find myself in such a place!

Colin's story

As luck would have it I had to pay it a visit to a sexual health clinic recently. For a variety of reasons that we don't have to go into here, I found myself sitting with a group of men early one morning in the waiting room of one of Glasgow's main clinics. This was a fascinating experience for me. I have to confess that I was completely ashamed at the thought of having to go at all - a shame that was clearly shared by my colleagues in the waiting room. Never was a copy of the daily paper or one's feet so closely examined! No eye contact made. No names mentioned. It was all very strange.

In the middle of all of it I felt a sudden urge to lead the group in a short reflection of how we got there and wanted to say that at least we were all there because we were having sex! That made me feel alive and cheerful. That may shock and offend you, but it's the truth.

Now as it turned out I was disease-free, and the time I spent with the doctor was actually quite pleasant and very useful! It clarified for me as a mature adult, that there are big gaps in my knowledge about sex and the hazards that go with it and that there's always a need to keep up to date with new developments.

It is helpful to look at the current statistics available from NHS Scotland's Information and Statistics Division and the Public Health Laboratory Service about the incidence and types of infection that people are getting today. The main types of infection are genital warts, genital herpes and chlamydia. How much do we know about these conditions - what they are and how one gets them?

Genital warts

The most frequently reported infection is genital warts. They are caused by the Human Papilloma Virus (HPV) and can appear anywhere on the genital and anal areas of the body. (In a very few circumstances they appear in the mouth, nose and throat.) Sometimes they are difficult to see and so people can be infected without really knowing, although the warts will most likely cause irritation of the skin. The main way of contracting genital warts is through skin to skin contact - using condoms doesn't help avoid infection. People aged 20-24 years are the most likely to contract genital warts. In 1999/2000 there were 5,433 diagnoses of first occurrence genital warts in Scotland.

Genital herpes

In Scotland, the incidence of genital herpes increased by 11.4% between 2000 and 2001, with recurrence rates rising by 12.1%. In 2000 around 17,000 people throughout the UK experienced their first attack and sought advice and help from their local STI clinics. Genital herpes is a condition that can never be completely got rid of, as the virus which causes it remains in the body once contracted. The initial attack can be very painful and subsequent attacks less so. The main symptom is fluid-filled blisters which burst and cause pain. Treatments can reduce the pain and discomfort, but the main way of dealing with this condition is to look after yourself by having a healthy diet and avoiding too much stress.

Chlamydia

The incidence of chlamydia is increasing. In Scotland it rose from 1637 cases in 1995/6 to 3497 cases in 1999/2000. In 2000 there were over 39,000 cases in England, Wales and Northern Ireland amongst young people aged 16-24. The main symptoms of the disease in the early stages are the abnormal discharge of pus or mucus from the vagina or penis, and pain while urinating; if left untreated, chlamydia can cause more lasting problems, including infertility. One of the key problems here is that people can have chlamydia and not be aware of it, which is one of the reasons why its incidence is increasing. I worked with a young man who discovered he had this disease and was advised that he would have to contact any sexual partners because they would need to be tested and treated if necessary. He had had no idea that he was infected.

Gonorrhoea

This STI is making a comeback.[1] In Scotland the incidence of gonorrhoea had reduced dramatically between 1985 and 1994 when there were just 272 cases. This figure has slowly begun to rise again and the most recent figures suggest there were 586 cases. It is a bacterial condition, which if left untreated can cause serious problems for both men and women. The most common symptoms are unusual discharges from the vagina or penis and pain when passing urine; again, some people will be unaware that they are infected. In 2001 in England 22,116 cases were identified, an 8% increase on the previous year.[2] The highest rates of gonorrhoea are seen in women aged 16-19 and in men aged 20-24 years.

Syphilis

The incidence of syphilis is also increasing. In 2000 there were 322 cases throughout the UK but in 2001 that number had increased to 697. Syphilis is passed on very easily through vaginal, anal or oral sex. Initial symptoms include sores on various parts of the body which if left untreated can fade but will be replaced by a non-itchy rash over the body. If left untreated the consequences can be very serious. The disease can lie latent in the body for up to 10 years before having a devastating effect on the brain, heart and liver.

Help available

The BBC has a very useful website with very clear information and advice about STIs and many other sexuality related issues: www.bbc.co.uk/health/sex. But beware, some of the photographs aren't for the faint-hearted. It's worth visiting the site if you are a parent or a youth worker, or just if you're living with your own questions about sex or sexuality. I once visited a sexual health clinic designed specifically for young people, and the key issue that emerged in discussion was that people contract STIs because they do not know how to avoid them. It would seem that in spite of living in a highly sexualised culture where sex is apparently freely available, we are not good at safe sex.

Talking about sexuality

Again this points to an issue of vocabulary. The church is one of the biggest providers of youth work in the UK and in many other countries, yet how many churches would be brave enough to talk to young people about such issues? How many youth workers are even able to give young men and women information about how to use a condom properly - which could reduce the potential for the development of some of the diseases listed above?

---

[1] Information and Statistics Division, NHS Scotland, 2002

[2] Public Health Laboratory Service, 2002

Gaps in our vocabulary mean that we do not know how to talk about sexuality. This perpetuates a culture where sex is still seen as a furtive and taboo subject. We do not celebrate sex in our culture, we demean it, we trivialise it and we reduce it to a physical act devoid of feeling. The churches are supposed to be connected to the Creator who is given the credit for having invented sex - and yet they seem to be either very quiet about the finer points of the safe sex agenda, or else are consistently giving out the 'don't do it' message. Do you believe God invented sex? If so, isn't it worth celebrating and rejoicing and creating a whole new positive dynamic which recognises the spiritual dimension alongside the physical? I think so. If we were to do that, then it's just possible that the incidence of STIs might fall.

The continuing and global HIV/AIDS pandemic

We have all been living with HIV/AIDS for more than 20 years. When the stories about the disease began to emerge in the press and on television, this seemed to be located specifically within the male homosexual community in the United States. Now it is a worldwide problem - particularly in parts of Africa where the numbers of infections and deaths are so high that it is difficult to take them in.

In the West the appearance of 'combination therapies' using a finely-tuned cocktail of drugs has been very successful in slowing down the development of the diseases associated with AIDS. For some people, the effects of the virus almost disappear. However, in parts of Africa, governments have had to fight to get drugs at a price they can afford for the millions of people who are infected with the HIV virus.

In the UK there are concerns that the success of the new drug therapies has resulted in reduced vigilance in relation to safer sex. According to Crusaid, a leading campaigning organisation in the UK, the number of people living with HIV rose by 11% in 2001. Since the early 1980s, more than 14,000 people in the UK have died. In the third world the numbers are in the millions.

It is particularly important not to get into a debate that is influenced by notions of HIV/AIDS 'victims' being either "deserving" or "undeserving". I say this because I sense that while people are in general terms sympathetic to the plight of those suffering from HIV/AIDS in the African continent, there seems to be less sympathy for people closer to home who are living with the virus. The logic here seems to be that people in the developed world 'should have known better'! I find it hard to imagine that Jesus would make such a distinction; I don't think he would even see it.

Why are we so frightened to discuss sex and to practise safe sex? Why are we so reluctant to admit that people are having sex regularly? How many more people will die before we take our responsibilities in this area seriously?

Teenage pregnancy - myth and fact

According to One Parent Families Scotland, there has been remarkably little growth in the incidence of teenage pregnancies in the last 20 years. When we consider some of the reporting on this issue we might think that the opposite is true. OPFS says that young women under 20 years of age account for only 3% of lone parent families in Scotland. Let's consider some further facts:

❖ 75% of teenage mothers register the birth jointly with the baby's father and the great majority of these couples are cohabiting. This goes some way to dispel the myth about such births happening because of teenage promiscuity.

❖ Marrying while pregnant is less common than in years gone by. Today 80% of babies born to the under twenties are to unmarried parents; but marriage does not necessarily indicate a stable relationship, as 46% of marriages fail when one or both parties is under 21 years old.
(One Parent Families Scotland, 2002)

The tabloid press and some political groups put forward the image of the loose-living, determined 15 year-old woman who decides to get herself pregnant so that she can have her own ready-furnished home for free - all at the tax-payer's expense. The reality would seem to be very different.

When I visited the sexual health facility for young people in Glasgow one of the key issues for the young women who used the service seemed to be a lack of self-esteem. Many young women said that they had become pregnant unintentionally, but had been willing to take the risk because they thought the man they were having sex with really did love them. Because of their low self-esteem they had not insisted on using condoms and had also put themselves at risk of STIs.

There are key issues here that will influence our developing vocabulary. Sex isn't just about physical mechanics or safety, it's also about our sense of who we are and how much we value ourselves and one another. How do we help young women with low self-esteem say 'no' to a persistent young man who threatens to withdraw his affections if they don't have sex? How do we help young men to value young women as human beings and not as conquests? These are key issues. Mistakes made at this age can have long-lasting and devastating effects. Becoming a parent is just one of them. When a young woman does get pregnant, the church should be on hand to offer as much support as possible. It should recognise that the young woman has a choice - to keep her baby or to terminate her pregnancy should she wish to do so. The late Cardinal Winning, former leader of the Roman Catholic Church in Scotland, led a campaign to support such young women by providing financial help that would ease them through pregnancy and into parenthood. Many people criticised this approach because they felt that the church was pressurising vulnerable young women into making a choice which might not be the best for them by flashing money in front of them; but we should remember that we cannot affirm a woman's right to choose termination without equally affirming her right not to do so.

Conclusion

Our perceptions about sex and sexuality are subject to myth and moral panic. We often think things are much worse than they really are and respond accordingly. Instead of rolling up our sleeves and properly engaging with people in the discussion of these issues, the churches have taken a more distant approach. Perhaps this is because the Christian churches in the UK and most of Europe have been relegated to a more marginal position in secular, post-Christian society? Instead of recognising that this is a position from which to be radical and offer positive alternatives, the churches seem to be stuck in a groove - offering advice that seems largely irrelevant and pinning their colours to the 'ideal of marriage' mast.

We might also remember that while traditional understandings of marriage may seem to be less popular today, committed relationships abound and the majority of children are brought up in two-parent families. And where children are brought up in one-parent families it does not necessarily follow that they will be emotionally, psychologically or in any other way disadvantaged.

A key issue for the churches is how to prepare their own communities to be sexual beings. How do we help each other to understand and discuss our sexualities? Another key issue for discussion is how we might contribute to the 'village' idea. How do we support young married couples, or parents with children, or same-sex couples, or older people? Do we want to provide a supportive and nurturing village, or do we think we have a right to be judgmental? Worse, would we rather pretend that nothing uncomfortable was happening at all and just ignore any difficulties?

In relation to the issue of sexuality, the churches' sanctuaries have become their prisons. So many church people are hermetically sealed off from real life. They are in danger of being proud of living a life that is 'better' than the lives of others.

Lazarus' story
There was a rich man who was dressed in purple and fine linen and lived in luxury every day. At his gate was laid a beggar named Lazarus, covered with sores and waiting to eat the food

which fell from the rich man's table. Even the dogs came and licked his sores.

The time came when the beggar died and the angels carried him to Abraham's side. The rich man also died and was buried. In Hell, where he was in torment, he looked up and saw Abraham far away, with Lazarus by his side. So he called to him, 'Father Abraham, have pity on me and send Lazarus to dip the tip of his finger in water and cool my tongue, because I am in agony in this fire.'

But Abraham replied, 'Son, remember that in your lifetime you received your good things while Lazarus received bad things, but now he is comforted here and you are in agony.'

Luke 16:19-25 (NIV)

How appropriate this story is. It's a reversal of fortune story, surprising to those who heard it because the outcome was not to be expected nor would it have been in alignment with religious views and practice of the day. In Jesus' time the religious and the wealthy lorded it over the ordinary, the poor and the sinful. There is a danger that this is happening again today. This story from the New Testament is a warning to us.

The church urgently needs to develop a new vocabulary for talking about sex. We need to rediscover how to talk to people about marriage, divorce, gay sexuality, living together, parenthood, singleness, or celibacy. In having these conversations both inside and outside the walls of the church we will learn a lot about how people really live today, their hopes and fears, aspirations and concerns.

In the Church of Scotland many congregations are trying to discover and understand how our lives together might look if we were to become a 'church without walls' [3] This process, approved by the General Assembly of 2001, encourages congregations radically to reform their lives and ways of worship and living together so that the witness of the body of Christ is seen by the community around us - so that the imprisoning sanctuary becomes instead the launchpad for new missionary zeal and activity in the places where we live. It is vital we do this. If we do not, we will continue to be alienated from the vast majority of the people in our communities and so will continue our descent into irrelevance.

The church needs salvation today. It needs to be saved from its fear, its disgust, its moral superiority and its ignorance. It needs to have these conversations with its people. In doing so it will offer salvation to them and find it for itself.

[3] Report of the Special Commission Anent Review and Reform; *Reports to the General Assembly of the Church of Scotland 2001*, reprinted as *Church Without Walls*, Parish Education Publications 2001; See website, www.cofscotland.org/churchwithoutwalls

chapter 5

Unlocking the closet

Hearing new voices

A few years ago I ran a conference for youth workers in the Church of Scotland on issues of sexuality. We called the conference 'Unzipped' and on the publicity we had a close-up photo of a pair of unzipped jeans. We hoped that the conference would create a new space in which different kinds of conversation could happen about issues that the church traditionally has problems discussing.

The day left me with a number of impressions. The first was just how naïve I was in thinking that we could achieve that new space in one day. I was also struck by some feedback from one of the young gay men in the group. He had attended one of the sessions led by staff from a voluntary sector organisation dedicated to helping young people with issues of sex/sexuality, and as a warm-up exercise the members of the group had been asked to tell the whole group the name of the first person they had ever fancied. He was instantly put in the uncomfortable position of either having to tell a lie or outing himself in what might very well be (and probably actually was) a fairly hostile group. I learned that day why it is important for us to think through these kinds of encounters so that we don't make those kinds of mistakes.

The main issue that I took away from the day was one presented by members of staff based in a sexual health and education agency in Inverness. They had come to the event hoping that the Church was going to say something new and useful about sexuality. I suspect they were disappointed. However, while they may have gained little from the conference, I gained a lot from them.

During one session I was leading, the staff from the agency mentioned that a problem they were dealing with regularly involved gay and lesbian young people who had a church connection. They said that these young people often came to them in distress, experiencing a Herculean struggle between their sexuality and their faith. The young people seemed to think that they could be *either* Christian or *gay*, but that they couldn't be both. Either way they were left with a sense of losing something very important to them. Something that was part of their fundamental identity.

At that time I was working on a Masters Degree programme and had been thinking about what to do for my dissertation topic. I had settled on research into the impact of training on youth workers but when I heard these stories from Inverness I decided to go down a very different route.

The new route was one that I had never anticipated and I could not have known that I would end up writing this book as a result. But at that point - around five years ago - I stood on the edge and had no idea where to go next. While I had anecdotal evidence from the project in Inverness, how exactly would I go about 'proving' that the church is a hard place to be if you are young and gay? And how exactly might I find young gay and lesbian people in an institution like the Church of Scotland? I realised very quickly that it was unlikely they'd be queuing up to speak to me!

I started to read. And quickly I began to hear voices that I hadn't known were there. This one in particular struck me early on because it articulates quite beautifully the pain and struggle faced by young people who are gay and who also have a Christian faith.

A young man's story

I am a young gay Christian who is struggling to come to terms with not only my own sexuality but also with the church's confusing teaching on this issue at the present time. A small proportion of my friends know that I am homosexual but the majority of these are non-Christians. I don't feel that I can tell my Christian friends because I think that I am going to get a bad and unsupportive reaction from them.

At the moment I just feel really isolated as even though I know other gay people, none of them are Christians and therefore cannot understand the difficult position I am in. I feel that I am being torn in two completely different directions, in one direction by my faith and in the other by the way I feel towards my sexual preference. Mostly I feel I have got it sorted out with God, but then God is a lot more understanding than I know that some of my friends are going to be.

(S Gill 1988, page 113)

These words - if we really listen to them - say an enormous amount to us about what the church really is today. This young man's experience also chimes with those of others included later in this book.

Can you feel the sense of isolation this young man feels? What must it be like not to be truly known by people who are important to you? What must it be like to feel that if you were known by them they wouldn't want to know you? What must it be like to feel as though you are being torn in two?

And what must it be like for a young person like this to hear these words from a very senior and well-respected churchman: 'The Church's condemnation is of homosexual practice not the homosexual person. We recognise that homosexual feelings exist and, although disordered, are not sinful per se' (Cardinal Thomas Winning, *Scotland on Sunday*, 7 November 1999). Is this young man's struggle not bad enough in and of itself, without the pain of hearing that that side of him is 'disordered' and that any activities related to that disorder are condemned by the church?

So my course was set. I decided that this was an area of enquiry worth exploring, and that the key questions I faced at the time were these:

- Is the Church of Scotland the kind of community in which gay and lesbian young people feel that they belong and can play a full part?

- Does the Church of Scotland align itself with those who feel a sense of unease about homosexuality, or is it openly supportive towards gay and lesbian people and issues?

- How does any position taken by the Church of Scotland on homosexuality affect gay and lesbian young people?

- Are gay and lesbian young people well supported when they turn to ministers, other Church members or personnel or other young people?

At the time I felt I could answer all these questions without further research! However, it was important to back up the stories that were being told with harder evidence. More importantly, it was time to listen to a part of the church community that hadn't been listened to; time to help that voice to be heard.

In a recent study produced into the needs of young gay, lesbian and bisexual people for the Greater Glasgow Health Board, 16% of the young women questioned and 7% of the men had been harassed or faced violence in either a church or another place of worship.[1] Bearing in mind that only a minority of the people questioned would have had any associations with a church or other place of worship, these figures, though small, probably represent a significant number of those who had such an affiliation.

This links with one of the stories told to me by one of the young people I interviewed as part of my research. He tells of a time when he was new to his church and was involved in a small study group with some other adults. He had only just found faith at a mission event and this group seemed to be an important part of how he was working out his first steps of faith. He may have become more open about his sexuality or perhaps it was simply 'found out' by members of the group, by which time he had already spoken to his minister, who had been supportive. The young man then related an experience with one member of the group who had a problem with his sexuality - an experience which became pivotal in his walk with Jesus. 'One communion we had she said she couldn't take communion with me. She said it wasn't anything to do with me and she still cared about me, but I thought, what is that all about?'

This was his first encounter with any kind of negative reaction to his sexuality. He was 17 years old and this experience made him decide to leave that church and seek a safer space. He found that space in another church in a completely different denomination, where he is now being encouraged to offer himself for full-time ordained ministry.

Can you imagine how difficult this experience must have been for the young man? Can you remember the days when faith was young and fresh for you and things were

[1] *Something to Tell You - A Health Needs Assessment of Young Gay, Lesbian and Bisexual People in Glasgow*, Greater Glasgow Health Board, May 2002

important and vital? Was it right for the woman to say that she couldn't take communion because he was there? Sadly, the young man looked to his minister for support on that occasion but the minister remained silent. Doubly betrayed, the young man saw no real option but to go elsewhere.

This is an example of what Petrovic refers to as 'redemptive violence'. 'The redemptive violence… is particularly evident vis-à-vis gay and lesbian students. By this I mean that violence (physical, emotional, and spiritual) is used against gay and lesbian students in an effort to force their own redemption. In this process, God is often used to support hateful positions. The problem is that the purveyors of these positions see them not as hateful but loving and caring' (Petrovic 2000, page 51). In the situation involving the young man and his housegroup, the woman who refused to take communion with him felt she was offering care by extending a hand to save the young man from his 'condition'. Redemption is possible, but on someone else's terms. That someone else is obviously purported to be God and has nothing to do with the prejudice of the mouthpiece.

Creating the space for voices to be heard

After my experiences above, in approaching the writing of this book I consulted widely with individuals and organisations relating to these issues. I met with the workers of the sexual health and advice organisation who had contributed to my appreciation of the problem - and with representatives of the Presbyterian Church in the United States of America, a sister denomination of the Church of Scotland that is also struggling with gay and lesbian issues. I also attended the Lesbian and Gay Christian Movement conference held in Edinburgh in June 2000. I also had conversations with colleagues in Scotland, Canada, Germany and Sweden. These meetings helped to shape and reshape the central themes of this book.

However this was not enough. All these conversations could do was to help illuminate the problems in general and to add to the anecdotal evidence. I knew that for this book to offer anything of substance I would have to speak to the main players in this story - ministers, youth workers, young people and more specifically gay and lesbian young people.

Turning the key

In asking these questions it was clear that as well as focusing on the specific experience of gay and lesbian young people, questions about views on homosexuality would have to be asked of the wider church. I knew that this would have to be done sensitively and that it might prove difficult to get people to answer any enquiry I made of them. The biggest problem was trying to locate gay and lesbian young people who were still involved in the Church of Scotland or at least still had some kind of residual contact with it.

In the end I decided to send out questionnaires to a small sample of ministers, youth workers and young people to test the pulse of the church at a particular point in time. I knew this would not prove to be an exhaustive or definitive study but rather one that would give a glimpse of where the church was 'at' with these issues at a that moment in time. I also began to track down some young people with relevant experience, and eventually managed to find seven brave souls who were willing to meet with me and talk about their lives. This process seemed to me to offer the widest and most representative range of the church's views while also providing some in-depth individual experiences.

Ministers

I contacted ministers to find out about their general views on homosexuality and, specifically, whether or not gay and lesbian young people had turned to them for support at any point in time.

Questionnaires were sent to a number of ministers on the current list of serving ministers, one randomly selected from each Presbytery (collection of local churches) in the Church of Scotland. This provided a geographical spread across Scotland. Slightly under half of the ministers responded and another sent back his questionnaire uncompleted, encouraging me to 'abandon' the research because he considered it to be 'pointless'. Unfortunately, due to the random process of selection, very few of the ministers contacted were women, so the vast majority of the responses were from men. This proved to be an unexpected bonus as research by the Terrence Higgins Trust had suggested that men find dealing with these issues more difficult than women; so the fact that the vast majority of ministers who responded were men was, in fact, an advantage in terms of illuminating the state of play in an organisation as peculiar and male-dominated as the Church of Scotland. But this does also point out the need for a further, gender-balanced examination of this issue in churches with female clergy.

Youth workers

I contacted youth workers for the same reasons as the ministers. It would be interesting to see if young people were more likely to turn to them for support rather than their ministers.

The Church of Scotland has a network of paid youth workers who work in local churches and other organisations in various locations around Scotland. Around 40% of the workers I contacted responded; I was disappointed in this response, as I assumed that because this group was working closely with young people they would be interested in the purpose of my enquiry.

Young people

It was important to involve young people in this part of the study for a number of reasons - to find out their views on homosexuality, to find out whether they had provided support at any time to a gay or lesbian young person and to see if age makes a difference in terms of theological views and the possibilities for providing support.

I worked with a group of 35 young people aged 18-25 gathered in Edinburgh from all over Scotland in May 2000 to take part in the General Assembly of the Church of Scotland. This was a captive audience of young people with a particular commitment to and involvement in the Church of Scotland. However, I felt it was appropriate to involve this group because it was a fairly diverse in terms of church background and experience as well as geographical spread, so as to get comparable answers. It was also a group that was well versed with the issues and possibly more articulate in framing responses.

There was a huge response from this group, which was interesting and encouraging. Most interesting of all, 4 of the young people chose to identify themselves as gay or lesbian. This was incredibly helpful as it provided my first glimpse into the secret world of gay and lesbian young people in the Church.

The first glimpse through the door

· ·

The purpose of asking these questions was to try to determine the nature of the church context for gay and lesbian young people. What would ministers, youth workers and other young people think about homosexuality? Would they have experience of gay and lesbian young people being part of their congregations? Would they think that their congregations would welcome openly gay and lesbian young people? The answers to these questions were in a way unsurprising, but still shocking - as we will see in the next chapter.

chapter 6

Welcome

to Narnia

· ·

What did people say?

The main questions I asked all of
those I consulted - ministers, youth
workers and young people - related
to their theological views on
homosexuality: is it 'allowed' or not,
and if it is allowed, then how much?
The second main focus I asked them
to consider was whether or not they
felt that their congregations would
welcome an openly gay or lesbian
young person.

The theological issues

On the question of whether homosexuality is 'allowed', there was a 50/50 split. Half the people responding had positive views about homosexuality and half had negative views. On the surface, then, we might be tempted to think that on the whole this is a pretty good result for gay and lesbian young people. It does indicate that grounds may exist for hope within the gay and lesbian community of the church. However a closer examination of the responses shows some serious underlying issues:

- Sixty-two per cent of the ministers who responded chose the negative options to answer this question, suggesting that ministers in the Church of Scotland might hold mainly negative views about homosexuality. Since they have the primary pastoral and leadership roles in local churches, this could represent a real problem in the provision of helpful support for gay and lesbian young people.

- Half the youth workers who responded did so from within the less positive options. Again this suggests that another group potentially in the position of offering support to gay and lesbian young people would do so from a negative theological standpoint, though not to the same extent as ministers.

- Looking at the figures for the young people it can be seen that the overwhelming majority of the young people questioned fit into the more positive categories. This confirms the information provided by the Terrence Higgins Trust suggesting that young people are more likely to be open to this issue than older people. Had it not been for the more positive response of the young people in this part of the study, the results in this section would have made very depressing reading indeed from the point of view of the gay and lesbian members of our church community.

Belonging to a local church

I asked respondents to give their opinion on how easy or otherwise it might be for an openly gay or lesbian young person to be involved in their congregations. The responses suggest that in the opinion of the vast majority of the respondents (77%) the church is either a 'not very easy' or a 'very difficult' place for gay and lesbian young people to be openly involved.

Before drawing conclusions about what has been discovered so far, time needs to be spent looking at the results found within each group.

The views of ministers

It was interesting that ministers were the only group that had had any significant contact with gay and lesbian young people. Five of the ministers who responded (24%) had had contact with a gay or lesbian young person. From this group it emerged that the ministers themselves had been involved in providing support in three of the cases, with other church members involved in the other two cases. All three ministers who had been approached for support from a gay or lesbian young person believed that homosexual practice is forbidden.

Of the ministers who had more positive views about the issue, the majority suggested that it would not be easy for a gay or lesbian young person to be open in their church. Some of the reasons given for this were:

- 'Most members would be reluctant to express a view and, more important, to go out of their way to befriend such a person. Some would object on Biblical grounds.'

- 'I feel that a gay or lesbian young person would be accepted by some but not all, and might very well experience coolness if not actual hostility.'

- 'In my experience, the majority of members of my congregation have very traditional views on homosexuality - that the practice is wrong and even, in the view of some, the orientation is wrong.'

It is clear from these comments that even in a situation where a gay or lesbian young person encounters a minister with positive views about homosexuality, the minister may be constrained by the wider congregation's perspective on the issue. The minister may simply feel that he or she is not allowed to be supportive.

Three of the ministers, however, suggested that it would be 'very easy' or 'easy' for gay and lesbian young people to be involved in their congregations. One suggested that it would be easy if the gay or lesbian young person was celibate, and another said, 'Ninety-nine per cent of the congregation is open and tolerant towards gays and lesbians, and our atmosphere in the church is warm, friendly and loving to all.'

The views of youth workers

An interesting feature about the people who responded from this group is that the gender balance was almost the exact opposite of that of the ministers' group, with the large majority being from women. This may indicate that more women serve as youth workers in the Church of Scotland than men; and if it is true that women in general terms are more open about homosexuality, then this might mean that youth workers would be a more supportive group for gay and lesbian young people.

In those who responded, though only a small number, there was a nearly 50/50 split in terms of theological views - very different from what we've observed above in the ministers' group. This would seem to support the possibility that youth workers, perhaps because they are working alongside young people, have more open views about issues of sexuality. Other considerations might include the fact that they are engaged with young people in an educational endeavour, and that perhaps implies that those who work in such areas lean more naturally towards more liberal views. Or perhaps it's a factor of age, social class - even the maternal instinct? The results are interesting as they stand now, but suggest other areas which it would be interesting to explore, outwith the confines of this present book.

Unfortunately, none of the youth workers who responded had had any direct experience with gay or lesbian young people. It may be that because the minister is so visible within a local congregation, she or he is the automatic first choice for young people to speak to. The majority of youth workers however suggested that it would not be easy for gay and lesbian young people to be open about their sexuality in their congregations. The reasons for this are summed up in the following comment:

'Most folks claim they'd be accepting but I don't believe they would find it as easy as they say. And if I don't, then it's highly unlikely that a young person in that kind of situation will either.'

Looking at the testimony from both the ministers' and youth workers' groups, there is an air of provisionality about the welcomes being extended to gay and lesbian young people. It seems as if what is being said is, you are welcome - but ...! Petrovic's work (see page 45) would suggest that people are engaged in a process where gay and lesbian young people can be included, but on the terms of the heterosexual majority and within a view that 'homosexuality is evil and sinful'. This would explain the provisional nature of the welcome extended to gay and lesbian young people in the Church context.

The views of young people

Something that is initially surprising in the views offered by the young people in response to these questions, is the fact that apart from the four forms returned by gay or lesbian young people, only one of those replying reported having any experience of a gay or lesbian young person being present within the church context. It is particularly interesting since this evidence is coming from within a group where at least four of its number were gay or lesbian. Perhaps for some of the reasons listed in the sections above the gay and lesbian young people in this group chose to remain hidden in terms of their sexuality.

The majority of young people had more positive views about homosexuality than either the ministers or the youth workers. However, again the majority suggested it would be very hard for a gay or lesbian young person to be openly involved in their congregations. Some of the reasons why are listed below:

- 'Our minister and his beliefs.'

- 'Lack of diversity in the congregation.'

- 'I think that the reaction of a lot of people in the congregation would have would be to condemn them and quote hellfire and damnation to them.'

However, it should also be noted that four of the young people suggested that it would be 'easy' for a gay and lesbian young person to be openly involved in their congregations. This was due to a 'younger minister' or a sense in which everyone was valued for 'who and not what they are'.

Other interesting things to emerge from the youth questionnaires were the fact that the young people seemed to have fairly definite ideas about homosexuality and none of them chose to hit the don't know box when asked about their theological views, and that none of them believed that homosexual orientation was sinful. The young people seemed fairly definite about what they thought. Might this suggest that the current generation of young people in the Church of Scotland could build a more open and tolerant Church in the future?

The views of gay and lesbian young people
As mentioned above, four young people in the group participating in the General Assembly of the Church of Scotland chose to complete the version of my questionnaire designed specifically for gay and lesbian young people.

The views expressed by these young people further illuminate all the evidence that has appeared so far. In the group of four there were two men and two women. Two believed the Church of Scotland's view on homosexuality was that it is possible to be gay, but that it is not permitted to participate in gay sex. One suggested that it was up to the individual to do what he or she sees fit, and the final member of the group said that they did not know what the Church's view was.

Two members of the group had approached someone in their congregations for support and had found this to be helpful. In each case, the person approached was a youth worker. The young people affirmed that it was meaningful to them to talk to someone who was 'genuinely interested' and who gave them a reassurance that they weren't 'odd'. The fact that the person they approached in each case was a youth worker might be significant, as we have seen from the results and discussions above that youth workers may be identified as being more positive about gay and lesbian issues. This links with the work carried out by Community Education Validation and Endorsement[1] in terms of values: specifically that one of the key community education

[1] CeVe, the body with devolved powers from the Scottish Executive to set professional standards in community education training programmes in Scotland, Guidelines for Pre-qualifying Training, Edinburgh, 1995

values is to 'respect the individual' and the individual's right to make his or her own choices. The responses from the young people here suggest that this fits what they experienced, and explains why the encounters were helpful.

On the question about whether or not their congregations would accept and support an openly gay or lesbian young person, all four suggested that it was not possible. Some of the reasons they gave are as follows:

- 'Recent press coverage has answered that one for me.'

- 'Because of the area that I come from, lesbianism is a big 'no thank you, we don't want to know' issue. Since homosexuality is not dealt with in the community, it is not something the church has to deal with, although I know how many would react as I have heard comments and it would not be welcoming.'

- 'Very traditionalist - "heterosexual family values are the only true way" - A very inhibiting, inhospitable place for young gay Christians.'

- 'Myself and two other "out" young people in my church have basically been told that we're welcome to come along, but the majority of the congregation want nothing to do with us.'

When asked what changes could be made to improve the situation for gay and lesbian young people in the Church of Scotland, some of the suggestions were:

- 'Acceptance and understanding - even just tolerance would do.'

- 'Recognition of homosexual relationships as being equal to that of heterosexual relationships. The Church needs openly to accept young gay people as part of the Christian community.'

- 'The Church of Scotland needs more leaders who are openly gay or lesbian or at least willing to stand up and say that they accept gay people in the church. Young gay people need role models.'

- 'A radical rethink - i.e. not just use the Bible as the rulebook of life - just as a guidebook.'

Asked how likely these things are to happen in the future, the young people appear to be less than optimistic, with one saying yes, another one no and two saying they don't know. The young people seem to sense that they are asking the Church to go beyond where it is comfortable on this issue. This matches fairly clearly with the responses from the other groups questioned, as examined above. The Church of Scotland doesn't appear to be ready to hear these suggestions yet, let alone form a positive response to them.

It is thus clear from this information that the Church of Scotland could have a problem with gay and lesbian young people. In the medium to long term it may be that the nature of the problem will change, since the youth of today's church seem to have more open views about homosexuality. This connects to ideas being explored by some in social science research, which point to the nature of exclusion as being 'dynamic' in its effects (Byrne 1999, page 1): Byrne's ideas point to the nature of exclusion as being 'dynamic' in the sense that it happens in a time and place in history, but that it is never static because we change our thinking about different issues. In the past women would have experienced exclusion in fairly dramatic ways but nowadays, while the problems have clearly not been completely solved, the extent of the exclusion experienced by women has changed. The implication of this is that while the Church of Scotland may have a problem with gay and lesbian issues today, it may not always have in the future. For gay and lesbian young people in the church today, it would seem that they might encounter very difficult views and opinions from people from whom they might expect support, and they might experience hostility within the membership of the church.

While the results so far suggest that there are genuine problems in the meeting of different mindsets, it is also clear that there are people in the Church of Scotland who want to be supportive and tolerant; there are churches that will provide a genuine welcome for young people. However, on the basis of this enquiry, the welcome might be scant in places.

Conclusion

The results of my investigation have given some genuine insights into the context that gay and lesbian young people experience in the Church of Scotland. The next section focuses on the interviews undertaken with seven gay or lesbian young people, whose experiences will provide a lot to this book. Not only does their experience illuminate for us an area of the church's life that has long remained in darkness, it points the way forward for the church in terms of dealing not just with the issue of homosexuality - or more importantly those within its ranks who are homosexual - but also to the issue that has driven this book so far: namely, how does the church respond to people who do not 'behave' conventionally in terms of sexuality and how do we develop new vocabularies to allow it to do so?

chapter 7

A *bruised*

reed

· ·

Interviews with gay and
lesbian young people

This chapter explores the results of a series
of interviews I held with gay and lesbian
young people, in which I asked questions
relating to their experience of being
homosexual and involved in the Church of
Scotland.

The numbers involved were small - as I
said earlier, it was hard to find young
people willing to take part - but the diverse
nature of the group in terms of age,
background, location and experience did
offer great potential. What the young
people said of their experiences, combined
with the findings and conclusions drawn
from the questionnaires discussed in the
previous chapter, gives us at the very least
some cause for concern and an agenda for
further consideration and possible action.

I made contact with young people through university chaplains, youth workers, other young people and colleagues. Some young people I approached refused to take part for fear that they would be 'outed', in spite of my assurances of confidentiality. It was particularly difficult to find young lesbians to take part. The profile of lesbians in the Church of Scotland seemed to be much lower than that of gay men. This may be a reflection of the wider gay and lesbian community where it seems that gay men are more visible and possibly better served by that community than lesbians - in which case, ultimately this may be more to do with gender and the needs of men to show off and be supported. Or perhaps more women have better supportive and nurturing relationships than men, and so have less need for a 'gay and lesbian community'. So overall, finding young people to offer personal testimony to this project took some considerable time - in itself an indication of what I was trying to find out.

The young people who agreed to meet me had all been or were all involved in the Church of Scotland in some way and were aged between 20 and 28. For reasons of confidentiality the names used are not the real names of the participants. I asked them the four key questions I had previously asked the ministers, youth workers and the wider group of young people (see page 48); we'll now look at these in turn, considering the responses the individual young people gave to each of these issues.

Is the Church of Scotland the kind of community in which gay and lesbian young people feel that they belong and can play a full part?

In terms of belonging, it is hard to say that the young people felt totally involved in the Church of Scotland; given that two of them have left it for another denomination (they both moved to the Scottish Episcopal Church), while two others left, one to stay outside the church altogether while the other returned to her local church after a gap of some years, only to leave again and remain outside. What made them choose to leave and move on?

In most cases the young people perceived that the Church of Scotland is, or was, saying two things at once - that it's okay to be gay but it's not okay to engage in any physical sexual activity. Many of them quoted the cliché 'hate the sin, love the sinner'. This provides a common thread of disappointment amongst the young people, who interpret this view as a lack of personal affirmation and welcome. They do not necessarily hear the positive part of the statement, or even feel indeed that this statement has a positive dimension at all.

It seems that the attitude summed up in the above statement does not help them to understand themselves. Robert, a 28 year old professional from Glasgow, said on this matter that he had at one time believed his sexuality to be wrong: 'I think I convinced myself that it was wrong but at the bottom of my heart I thought, this can't be wrong. How come if we are all created by this God, then why am I like this? I didn't choose this way.' He had questioned whether or not he was even 'worthy' enough to be allowed to serve in the local church.

Ben, an office worker from Glasgow aged 26, had an experience which connects with this, mentioned earlier in this book. He told me about a time when he was new to his church and was involved in a small study group with some other adults. This was an important part of how he was working out his faith. Remember his experience with one member of the group, 'One communion we had she said she couldn't take communion with me. She said it wasn't anything to do with me and she still cared about me but I thought, what is that all about?' This was his first encounter with any kind of negative reaction to his sexuality. He was 17 at the time and hadn't had any problems about his sexuality before coming to the church. As a result of this experience, he left that church to seek a safer space.

Justin, a professional from the Greater Glasgow area aged 26, commenting on the Church of Scotland's 'love the sinner, hate the sin' attitude, suggests that, 'You cannot say you're in sympathy with the core of someone's being and then say we don't like what they do, because what they do is inexorably linked to who they are.' It seems that it is easy in forming policy to separate orientation from practice, but when you are living as a gay or lesbian young person it is much harder to make that separation.

Alison was 24, from the Highlands and working in the tourist industry; she relates that, when trying to understand her sexual identity, she chose to leave the church she was attending rather than deal with the guilt she was feeling. Instead she talked to 'gay friends who weren't Christians and couldn't understand the guilt aspect, which is awful and still is.' Her conclusion about why she couldn't stay was, 'I didn't fit in.'

Fiona, a civil servant from Glasgow aged 22, approached her minister at a time when she was in a stable relationship. Her partner had started to accompany her to church, and she wanted to talk the situation over with the minister. 'I think I had just reached a point where I wanted to discuss it and get the opinion of someone that I actually did respect.' She goes on to say that the minister didn't seem to engage with her story, and this left her feeling that if the minister wasn't interested then no one would be. The minister's response wasn't the only reason she left the church she was attending but from what she said it seemed to be the main one. She is still very angry about this encounter; she had hoped for much more but was left feeling short-changed.

For these young people then, their experience of church has left them feeling excluded. Not only is there a sense of not being welcome, encounters with other church members actually hastened their departures.

But this phenomenon is not restricted to the churches. Conclusions drawn from research work into the experience of gay and lesbian young people in schools is directly relevant here: 'The results of systematic exclusion and systematic inclusion are the same. Both add to the message to gay, lesbian and bisexual students that a part of their identity should not and cannot be shared. Gay, lesbian and bisexual students are forced to act straight in order to fit in and often feel that there is nowhere to turn.' (Friend 1993, page 53) Another social scientist goes from this conclusion to use a comment from a school student who had taken part in a study on gay and lesbian issues in a school setting. 'School was a definite hell-hole … Like, you sit in class, right, and all these girls are talking about which boys they like and all that crap. And you make stuff up, like "Oh yeah, he's really cute. Yeah Tom Selleck, wow." You don't know how many times I wanted to lean over and say, 'hey, what about Julia Roberts? Some fox, huh?' (O'Connor 1994, page 9). The settings are different but the words of this young woman do chime with the words of the young people who took part in this project. There is the same sense of exclusion, the sense of something inside that was too big and too difficult to bring out into the open and the fear of being discovered and what that might mean.

If we accept, with current thinking,[1] that the marks of an inclusive community are:

- Integration
- Prevention
- Understanding
- Inclusiveness
- Empowerment

then it would seem that the church - nationally and locally - has failed these young people. Their experiences demonstrate an experience of what one writer calls 'systematic exclusion' and 'systematic inclusion' (Petrovic 2000). On the one hand there is an absence of positive discussion or any other form of visibility about issues surrounding homosexuality, and on the other hand an inclusion which is conditional and determined by a hostile community.

In contrast, the two young men who moved on to the Scottish Episcopal Church describe how they felt when issues of homosexuality were openly discussed. Robert describes his new church as 'a place where sexuality was talked about, particularly from the pulpit, and it was talked about more openly and it was talked about with … tolerance, compassion… and with affirmation. I found that there was this affirmation of who you were and it was okay to be who you were, and to explore who you were. And to develop as that.' He goes on to say that 'It was almost too good to be true.' Ben talked about working alongside an openly gay priest: 'There was a priest who was openly gay, and probably the most popular priest in the congregation, people were actively there, families were actively there because he was there. But not because he was gay. It just so happened that he was gay and most people were happy with that.' This was a positive experience for Ben's own journey. At this point there is a temptation to ask the question, is the Scottish Episcopal Church a haven for gay and lesbians in Scotland? It certainly seems so for these two young people.

[1] Social Inclusion - Opening the Door to a Better Scotland, Scottish Office, Edinburgh, 1999

Justin has been part of the same local church all his life and he seems to have found the most inclusive space of all the interviewees. It is interesting that he has experience of living in a mainly gay and lesbian community overseas, of which he says, 'to hear the words gay and lesbian affirmed in a worship service is very, very moving…that still haunts me.' It is clear that this experience of inclusiveness has helped him to stay within his local parish church and to be a force for change there.

He describes his local church as a safe space: 'I've been allowed to develop my faith through the people there.' However, in addition to this he was the only young person interviewed who had undergone any theological training, and it may be that this training (alongside the experience outlined above) gave him a more developed vocabulary and the confidence to deal with his own issues and the issues of the people in his local church.

It seems that at one and the same time, the church welcomes and rejects gay and lesbian young people. Some gay and lesbian young people are able to be open and involved in a local church, while others encounter indifference and hostility. Some are able to stay, some go.

The important discovery here is not only that the Church of Scotland is not inclusive for gay and lesbian young people. It is equally important to discover that it is possible for some churches to be inclusive in spite of the existence of policies that lead to exclusion. One writer suggests that in a large organisation or institution (such as the Church of Scotland), some people may not attach a positive 'meaning' to the organisation's official policy but go in a different direction altogether (D Silverman, 1970). This means that while there may be an impression that the Church of Scotland has endorsed a particular stand that forbids homosexual practice - mainly due to the nature of the debate so far and the theological perspective of the participants in it - some of the members of the Kirk may choose to ignore what they believe the the policy to be.

Does the Church of Scotland align itself with people who feel a sense of unease about homosexuality, or is it openly supportive towards gay and lesbian people and issues?
The interviews for this project took place while the debate about the abolition of Clause 2a (Section 28) was in full flow in Scotland. It proved very useful to ask the question about what the young people had 'heard' in the churches' contributions to the debate which dominated the Scottish political scene at that time. The responses indicate that key individuals in the Church of Scotland (and in other Christian denominations) have allowed the impression to develop that the Church is emphatically uncomfortable with the issue of homosexuality and with homosexual people.

While recognising that the churches have a right to a say in any debate on moral issues, Alison suggests that: 'It's fine and dandy for them to have their points of view, but unless they are struggling with their religion and sexuality they have no idea what they are really talking about.' She goes on to say, 'At least I know where I stand now, and I know it's something that can't be accepted in me.' There is a strong sense of finality expressed by her and others. It is as though a line has been drawn. They feel they are on the wrong side of the line.

Ben is particularly aggrieved with what he sees as the churches' complicity with wider, ignorant opinion, 'Some of the emotions I feel about it [the debate] are disbelief. What is this all about? Are people so naïve? What is it that is so threatening about gay people? Why are people so terrified?' He goes on to suggest that 'the marks of a dysfunctional society are old ladies being mugged in the street or houses being burgled or children being abused or a violent attack. Two gay men living in a suburban household with an estate car and a Labrador are not signs of a dysfunctional society.'

Throughout the interviews, the young people reported a range of emotions, from anger through to fear. Speaking of the contribution to the debate made by the late Cardinal Thomas Winning, former leader of Scotland's Roman Catholic community, Ben says, 'It is such an irony that he and people of the extreme right are talking together on this issue, when these people would normally never sit in the same room.' He goes on to suggest that the people from the churches who have been shouting loudest have been doing so not from real concern, but to pursue 'their personal hobbyhorse and personal phobias'.

Significantly, alongside the anger and fear one voice in the debate was singled out by the majority of the young people in a positive way. The Very Reverend John Cairns, Moderator of the General Assembly of the Church of Scotland in 1999, spoke out in favour of the repeal of Clause 2a, and was the only key religious figure to do so in such a public way.

John, who works in the financial services industry and lives in Tayside, sums up the response, 'I love John Cairns, because he has been so understanding and you think, yes, that's the way it should be.' However, the view from Fiona is that the existence of two opposing voices from the one institution is a sign of weakness: 'open a newspaper and the Moderator will say one thing and some other church figure will say another.' She feels that the Church has yet to take a clear stand on the issue. The recent stand-off between the current Moderator of the General Assembly, Right Rev Professor Iain Torrance and Rev Bill Wallace over the issue of the ordination of gay clergy in the Church of Scotland suggests that Fiona understands church politics on this issue only too well.

The story so far

From the evidence discussed so far, it would be hard to give the Church of Scotland a "gay-friendly" badge. The Church's contribution to the debate on the repeal of Clause 2a seemed, on balance, to alienate it further from these gay and lesbian young people.

Jesus Christ said, 'But if anyone causes one of these little ones who believe in me to sin, it would be better for him to have a large millstone hung around his neck and to be drowned in the depths of the sea' (Matthew 18:6).

Is the Church of Scotland open to gay and lesbian young people or not? If it is, then does the welcome come with strings attached? If the answer to that is 'yes', then we need to consider what that might mean, not just for gay and lesbian young people, but for all those whom the Church might deem to be 'badly behaved' in the realm of sexuality - those who are divorced, have many partners or are co-habiting.

There is a danger that if the Church attempts to withdraw the grace of God from people such as these, then it may be committing a grave error. It would do well to listen to the words of its founder, and ask itself some serious questions. This is not simply an issue about people who are homosexuals. This is an issue that affects all those who do not fit the stereotypes the Church has allowed itself to be imprisoned by. Something needs to happen - and fairly urgently - or eventually the Church will be very empty indeed.

Let's take time to pause for a moment and to let what you've read sink in for a while. Remember we are talking about real young people, not just statistics. Young people who have been growing up in congregations just like yours. Young people who have had to live with a sense of difference all their lives, and for whom the Church has not always been a safe place. They are our responsibility. They are part of our family. They are part of who we are. Will we accept or deny them?

chapter 8

Hearing the

voice of the church

Mixed messages?

There is obviously deep confusion about the Church of Scotland's policy on homosexuality. Robert says, 'I just think it is quite unclear', and this is echoed throughout the interviews. Now let's have a look at the rest of the interview questions.

How does any position taken by the Church of Scotland on homosexuality affect gay and lesbian young people?

Alison says that she has 'always been aware' of the Church of Scotland's views on the issue. Robert talked of an earlier debate at the General Assembly (in 1994), and expressed a sense of being 'disappointed and a bit lost' with the outcome. He said he was 'hoping that they [the General Assembly] would come out and say that it was okay'. The fact that they hadn't meant for him that he would have 'to struggle on trying to work it out for myself.' The way he worked it out was to go to a more accepting and affirming church in another denomination.

At least two of the young people suggest that in a sense it doesn't really matter what the institution says, the battles will be won or lost at a local level. Ben says, 'one of the difficult things for the Church of Scotland is the tension between a church which wants everybody to conform and a church that has a structure that is quite localised. So my understanding is that things would be very different from parish to parish.'

Ben goes on to say that 'the line is about trying to include and accept gay people within congregations but how do you do that? How do you accept someone by saying, you are welcome here but we don't really like what you do. That seems to be the line, certainly in official statements.' On hearing that 'official line' John said that he 'wanted to go running from the place.' He also goes on to say that he first became aware that the church had a problem with homosexuality when he was a teenager.

One of the interesting things is the way some of the young people have internalised the negative views to the extent that they use words like 'disgrace' (Robert) and 'disgusting' (Alison) to describe themselves. One of the saddest comments was made by Alison when she said, 'I know this is part of me and on a good day I know that God made me, but I really wish he hadn't.' She also tells of a time when she had sex with a partner and believed she 'was going to hell, literally in tears.' This young woman speaks of being so keen to become part of a new church she had chosen to attend, that she was prepared to give up her partner just to fit in.

Few of the young people interviewed fitted the caricature of the tragic gay or lesbian teenager desperately trying to understand him or herself. However, it is clear from the evidence that if these young people already have a negative view of themselves in terms of their sexuality, then the Church's official position (as communicated nationally and viewed by people locally) will add to their difficulties. This represents a double blow. The young people already know that they are different, they know that society doesn't always appreciate that difference and now it seems clear that the church really doesn't like it either.

This project shows that views expressed by the Church of Scotland and the way its members have treated four of the seven interviewees caused them to leave their churches. That is one serious consequence of the current position. The other main consequence is the distress that the official position causes gay and lesbian young people who are already trying to work out their sexual identities.

At the local level, most of the young people mentioned either the absence of discussion on the issue of homosexuality, or negative comments. Robert puts it this way, 'If it was talked about it was talked about in a negative way. There was never any positive talk about it.' Alison says that this negativity made her 'lead a double life'. She lived one life inside the church and another outside. This suggests that there is indeed a need for young people to be able to 'come out' for their own spiritual growth. Loranger, writing for a Jesuit publication, suggests there are some prerequisites which need to be in place before young people will trust a community with their inner worlds (M Loranger, 1997/90). It would seem from what the young people are saying here that the Church of Scotland is not providing that kind of opportunity for them. The consequences may well be damaging for them in the long term, if they are unable to be themselves within the church community. This can only be damaging for the church as well. If it is a place where people are expected to put on a face, or to live double lives, then who in their right minds would want to be part of it?

Are gay and lesbian young people well supported when they turn to ministers, other Church members or personnel, or other young people?

Most of the young people interviewed said they had tried to speak to someone within the church about their sexuality at some point in their teenage years. It seemed to be mainly ministers who were the first port of call, though not exclusively so.

Robert tells of approaching a minister from a neighbouring congregation because he thought he was a 'reliable guy'. Asked if this encounter was a helpful one he says, 'Sort of, yes he was understanding. He was supportive but in a kind of safe way.' He goes on to say that he felt the minister was quite guarded in his comments 'because he was unsure of what line he should take'. Others shared this impression, and felt that ministers' attitudes stemmed from fear of repercussions from their congregations and the church hierarchy. Such fears may not be unfounded. The Reverend Margaret Forrester's decision to bless a lesbian couple in the early 1990s seems to haunt her to this day and may well have caused her to lose out on the highest office of the Church of Scotland - that of Moderator of the General Asssembly.

This is borne out by the survey results showing that even ministers who had more open views about homosexuality felt that their congregations would not necessarily be a welcoming place for gay and lesbian young people. In such a situation it might be difficult for a minister to support a gay or lesbian young person for fear that it might provoke a backlash from his or her congregation.

Ben says that he didn't approach his minister for advice but because he wanted to be honest with him. (ministers or other church members should note that if approached by a gay or lesbian young person, they should not assume that support, advice and a shoulder to cry on is what is required.) Because of the hostility that Ben encountered in his bible study group, he hoped his minister might be supportive, and was disappointed when he was not. He felt that the minister was afraid to say anything in public that might be interpreted as being supportive. It is possible that this silence gave tacit approval to the woman who was refusing to have communion with Ben.

One of the effects of the Church of Scotland's position is that sympathetic ministers may not feel able to support gay and lesbian young people. There are echoes here from the repeal of Clause 2a - one reason for the repeal was that teachers felt constrained in supporting gay and lesbian young people in case they fell foul of the law.

Alison tells a related story. She had moved away from her home area and had left her local church but decided to go to another church, an independent evangelical fellowship. She quickly came to the conclusion that she could be part of the new church 'as long as I was quiet and didn't do anything and didn't share anything. And God's love would save me.' She feels that although this was a really negative situation, it did force her to make some positive choices for her life. She feels that she is in a better situation now, although her life no longer includes regular attendance at a local church.

Iain, a young man working in the hospitality industry in the West of Scotland and at 20 the youngest person to take part in the project, was aware of the risks attached to talking to anyone about his situation and has chosen not to tell anyone in the church but rather has sought help from people outside it. Ben talks about a similar experience with a teacher at school who was very helpful. These experiences suggest that the church is indeed a hostile place for gay and lesbian young people. For many of them the answer is either to speak to no one or to speak to a non-church person.

How can that be satisfactory? How can any of us - even those of us who are absolutely convinced of the rightness of our position on the wrongness of homosexuality - believe that this is what God wants?

Suggestions for change

A key part of the interview process was to ask young people how they thought the Church of Scotland could change, in order to improve the situation for gay and lesbian young people. Their suggestions were as follows:

1. The Church of Scotland should make a more positive statement about homosexuality.

2. The Church should create and support an agency that people can phone for advice and support.

3. There should be local support mechanisms - individuals who are sympathetic and who have listening skills and know how to respond sympathetically.

4. The church needs someone to champion gay people.

5. Establish a semi-autonomous network of gay and lesbian young people and people who would support them.

6. Admit that we are here.

7. Provide appropriate training for ministers, elders and others on how to deal with the issue.

8. Promote general awareness of youth issues - not only sexuality.

9. The Church of Scotland has to decide - do you want us here or not? If you do, then do something positive about it.

These suggestions are mostly fairly practical, and not outrageous. Some might present the Church with problems but, as Rabbi Alan Katz asserts, 'even if a religious institution is not favourable toward homosexuality it should be there to comfort and help the psychological healing of any of their members.' (Singer 1993, Page D-1) It seems, however, that the Church is caught in a dilemma. If it offers support to gay and lesbian young people, will the more conservative majority in the Kirk feel that this is undermining the Church's ideal of marriage? If it does nothing, then gay and lesbian young people will continue to find the Church a risky organisation to be involved with.

When asked how likely they thought it was that the Church of Scotland would make some of these changes, all the respondents said that they felt it unlikely. Justin puts it this way, 'The chances are fairly negligible. The Church of Scotland just isn't ready.' He suggests the real reason for this is because local churches aren't capable of having the discussions required to facilitate change, and that ordinary church members have no vocabulary to deal with this issue. He suggests that the consequence of this lack of progress will be that 'there won't be any gay and lesbian young people in the Church of Scotland because they'll leave.'

All the young people interviewed have had difficulties with the Church of Scotland - its views on homosexuality, its members and its general ethos. On the one hand, they see an ancient institution proud of its inheritance and place in society - a bastion trying to hold back the currents of moral crisis. On the other hand, there is a community within it seeking more visibility, asking to be valued, being treated badly and yet having the resilience in most cases to offer suggestions on how things could be improved. It is sad that the institution seems to kill off hope of change in the young people.

The leadership within the institution may feel that the Church of Scotland's perceived view is actually benign, and hope in some vague fashion that this will lead to the well-being of gay and lesbian young people. However, the Church may also be afraid to acknowledge and support those young people because this calls into question 'traditional values'. If the Church of Scotland changes its view on homosexuality - even a little - would that necessarily devalue the 'traditional' family? And even if the Church wanted to consider such an option, would this inevitably lead to schism - or the death of the Church as we know it? While change may be the inevitable result of such conflict, such change might not be positive for gay and lesbian young people. Yet should we not, in faith, take that risk?

Beyond all that are some simple facts. If we take this discussion out of the realm of theology, church policy and politics, and view it simply as a human rights issue, then surely we can see that the rights of these young people are being infringed? And if we asked people who are divorced, what might they say? Or people who are single or have chosen a celibate life? What about people who choose to live together but not marry? What about families who can no longer continue to be together and who separate? If we asked them similar questions what would they say? Do the churches afford them the same dignity and respect that they afford to people who are considered to be "well-behaved"? While the experience of gay and lesbian young people may evoke the most extreme response from an institution uncomfortable with difference, we cannot be naïve and fail to consider the possibility that what we are reading on these pages is the tip of a very large iceberg; and that our churches have many confused and hurting people in them for whom the church is a source of pain rather than solace. Worse still, there are many who represent the church in exile, who feel they can no longer continue a journey of faith within the walls of a local church because they cannot take their humanity into that building and they don't know where else to put it. But who cares? Do you?

Love and
marriage

One of the founding fathers of the Christian church, St Augustine, Bishop of Hippo, wrote, 'There is nothing which degrades the manly spirit more than the attractiveness of females and contact with their bodies' (Soliloquia 1.40). Surprised?

I was when I first came across these words. They are surprising because the Christian church today would have us believe that current constructs of marriage and family can trace their origins (without any breaks) way back into the historical mists of biblical times.

We live with what we know, and the churches know marriage. They know it inside out. They understand it. They set its limits, list its virtues and broadcast its ideals to the wider world. Marriage, as far as the churches are concerned, is good for you! More than that, marriage is the proper place for family, for the bringing up of children. As values go, that's a pretty potent one. Family = marriage.

However, there are difficulties with this point of view. Firstly, the institution of marriage as we have it today does not have an unbroken tradition stretching back into those mists. Secondly, people are increasingly bringing up children in non-traditional families. Thirdly, for a variety of reasons marriage is either not the favoured option of many heterosexual couples or, where it has been, it has ended in divorce.

Some interesting recent statistics:

- ❖ By 2005, Britain will have 1.7 million fewer people living as part of a family unit than in 2000.

- ❖ By 2005, Europe will have 11 million fewer people living as part of a family unit than in 2000.

- ❖ An additional 1.4 million couples will live together without having children.

- ❖ In 2000, thirty-seven per cent of the population of Europe lived as part of a nuclear family, but this will decrease to 34% by 2005.

- ❖ In 1970, there were 390,000 first-time marriages, in 1999 there were only 179,000.

- ❖ The proportion of women aged between 18 and 49 who were married fell from nearly three-quarters in 1979 to just over half in 2001.

- ❖ The trend of living alone has doubled in the last 40 years in the UK and today nearly one in three households are single occupation.[1]

These statistics must make us think about where our ideas about human relationships come from, and what we should do about organising them. Let's examine the foundations of marriage as we know it today. Are they in fact as we have been taught to believe?

'Either we marry to have children or, refusing to marry, we live in continence for the rest of our lives' (Justin Martyr, *Apology* 1:29). From this and similar statements made in the days of the early church, we discover that the nature and understanding of marriage at that time was somewhat different from today. Many sections of the early church were suspicious of the erotic in any form, and saw marriage simply as the means for procreation. Marriage was not about family, nor was it about sexual pleasure, it was

[1] From 'Single households set to soar', *The Guardian*, 27 November 2002 and 'From this day forward....', BBC News, 15 February 2002

simply for having children and continuing the human species.

Boswell suggests that, 'the most popular manual of moral doctrine in the Middle Ages cited both Pythagoras and Saint Jerome as insisting that "a man who loves his wife very much is an adulterer. Any love for someone else's wife or too much love for one's own is shameful. The upright man should love his wife with his judgement, not his affections."' (Boswell 1980, page 164, quoting Vincent of Beauvais). Early Christian thinkers seemed to have been deeply suspicious of love between men and women. This may well stem from a latent suspicion about women's power to ensnare men and imprison them forever.

The Rev Canon Dr Martyn Percy, director of the Lincoln Theological Institute at the University of Manchester, suggests that 'In our own time, we are tempted to visit sexual history though the sanitised eyes of our Victorian forebears: the appeal to a moral or spiritual "back to basics" ideology rests on this perspective' (Percy 1997, page 13). And that is exactly what has happened. Our understanding of marriage today, and all that stems from it, is a very modern one and has little to do with biblical standards. True, we can see the basis of what we understand as marriage in the Bible, but we can also see other expressions of sexuality that were apparently approved of in those days. Percy again: 'We know from Scripture that there were many different forms of family life expressed in orthodox Judaism. True, monogamy was common, but polygamy and concubines were not unknown, and their offspring were deemed ... to be legitimate heirs' ((Percy 1997, page 13). He goes on to suggest that children in these days were 'produced' to provide for one's old age. Who would look after you when you are old, if you didn't have children? Childless widows did not always fare well in such a culture.

In biblical times, marriage was fundamentally an arrangement between two families with little or no interference from outside parties. Nor did the people being married have much say in the matter. Often such arrangements were made for financial or wider economic, cultural or religious reasons. Therefore the tradition on which we stand is murky at best and downright confusing at worst.

Values - whether biblical or secular - are portable. They can be picked up and moved from one generation to another or they can be left behind - through choice or lack of use. This is what has happened to the 'rules' and expectations governing marriage. What we have today has little biblical, spiritual or ecclesiastical significance. Its significance lies in its legal status, and the values attached to it are clearly a social construction - which also has power to control behaviour.

The rules that govern marriage - whether the ones we have today or the ones we inherited from the days of old - do not necessarily fit our modern or post-modern culture. We have evolved as human beings. We are more independent and more solitary. We make decisions for ourselves and not always in the context of family. In the 'Christian West', we do not see any reason to organise marriage on an arranged basis.

Rather, we have decided that the supreme rule driving us towards marriage must be that of love - the very thing that the early Christian thinkers were deeply suspicious of.

The churches today clearly have to sort out what they mean by 'marriage'. We have to understand exactly what it is and the nature of its commitment, and then we need to decide how that commitment is to be demonstrated.

The Presbyterian Church in the USA (PCUSA) has defined marriage as follows:

> Marriage is a gift God has given to all humankind for the wellbeing of the entire human family. Marriage is a civil contract between a woman and a man. For Christians marriage is a covenant through which a man and a woman are called to live out together before God their lives of discipleship. In a service of Christian Marriage a lifelong commitment is made by a woman and man to each other, publicly witnessed and acknowledged by the community of faith.
>
> (PCUSA *Polity Reflections*, Note 42, 26 March 2001)

Such statements are helpful because they tell us what a church thinks marriage is and also what it is not. This statement tells us that marriage is a gift for everyone, that it is a gift from God. It then goes on to say that Christian marriage goes beyond this basic understanding because of the nature of the agreement between the man and woman directly involved and the community of faith surrounding them. This statement tells us who marriage is for and who it is not for. It is only for men and women. It is not permissible within this understanding for two men to be married to each other, or two women. This is where the statement's helpfulness starts to run out.

The growth of non-married partnerships has been steep. There have been increasing calls for - and now there is the possibility of - legal recognition of same-sex partnerships, and many more people are divorcing or choosing not to marry. These developments demand that we think. But what is the church to do? Can it be more inclusive and open to seeing that marriage in essence is about commitment between two people and the promises these two people make to one another? Here are two young people's experiences.

Graham's story

I was Project Leader for a youth work project. A number of local churches had got together to employ someone to work with the young people who they were not reaching with their traditional youth activities.

It was my first real job. I was 22 and engaged to be married. I lived too far away from my job to travel, so for a year I slept in a friend's spare room, ran up their phone bill and spent most of my minimal wage travelling backwards and forwards to see my fiancée. We had set a date for the wedding, one year from then. The strain of being apart was taking its toll, as was the drain on our finances paying digs and travelling every weekend. We decided that we should look for a flat, and we did. We moved in together. It wasn't a secret. We sought opinions on whether we were doing the right thing, and people were honest with us, some saying yes, some no.

Not long after we bought our flat, and my fiancée was lucky enough to get a job locally, a member of the management committee asked how we both were. I explained about our new home and her new job. He was less than pleased. He told me what I was doing was wrong and a bad example to the young people I was supposed to be serving. I had let them all down.

A meeting was called with all the various ministers and the management committee, twelve people in total, and me, alone. I was told by one person that I was unfit to work there and by another that I was a fornicator. I tried in vain to explain the circumstances, that we were committed to getting married and were committed to each other.

It was suggested that we get married as soon as possible to save any scandal. It was suggested that one of us move out of our home and live with someone else. I asked, given that we had been living together, had already had sex and were actually living in a committed monogamous relationship what doing any of these things would change. No answers came. I asked if marriage was more than a piece of paper to save scandal? No answers to that either.

Only one of the ministers, not my own, offered us any kind of pastoral support. He had made it clear that he did not agree with what we had done, but recognised that he still had a responsibility to care, and he did, and we were grateful.

In the end I was 'demoted'. My job title was changed from Project Leader to Project Worker and one of the ministers would not let me speak in his church. The project found out very soon that they had no grounds in law for disciplinary action. None of the young people I worked with ever commented on what I had done. No one in the churches I worked for ever commented, and we attended one of the churches regularly and were made welcome. It was never the same. I was so committed to the job and the people when I first took the post. I lost interest in the project, but not in the young people.

I remember a throw-away remark made by one of the ministers. He said at the end of my two-hour inquisition, 'This is nothing, you should see the fuss at the church up the road. They have a lesbian teaching Sunday School!'

I remember thinking how needless and pointless the whole thing was. It was never about discussion, even pastoral care. The whole crisis was driven by the fear of a scandal. I felt sad most of all. Sad at the inability of people to articulate their concerns, and to act in a concerned and pastoral way. Sad that they felt the need to judge our relationship without ever getting to know us.

My wife and I have been together for almost six years now. At that time she was just beginning to take an active part in church life. She is still uncomfortable in church. We had a two-year discussion about whether we should have our son baptised, mostly based on our concern about bringing a child into a community that thought the way those people did. In the end the *baptism took place with just a few friends and family there because we knew they would care about us and care for us.*

This is not an uncommon situation. It is unfortunate that the church could not recognise the commitment between these two young people - who had been together for a very long time and who had every intention of getting married. They key question for us all is when exactly does marriage begin? With the initial commitment or the public exchange of vows, or is it when two people live out their commitment to each other within the community which surrounds them?

We live in a day and age where marriage as we understand it is now easier to walk away from. This is the day of the 'no fault' divorce. Couples can divorce very quickly. Some would say that this has undermined the 'institution of marriage'. They may well be right but perhaps this is only because the way the institution was set up was fatally flawed, or perhaps it is because society has changed and people now want to change the ways in which they make relationships with one another.

Karen's story

When a marriage goes wrong it is a devastating blow akin to bereavement. The hopes and plans you made for your future together come crashing down amidst blame and hurt. It's all your fault, you've let people down, a failure. At least that's how it feels.

In church, a place where I expected forgiveness and understanding, I received awkward silences, lectures, judgement. The teaching was stacked against me. I didn't fit in. What was this terrible thing I had done? My life was in ruins, not at all how I'd planned it. I felt isolated and alone - all confidence gone. In the midst of that however, there were a handful of individuals who, like God, saw and loved only me.

When I joined the Church at 21 it was in the complete belief that God knew me and loved me for who I was. Why else would He freely give His only Son that all my past, present, and future sins would be forgiven? Divorce, and dealing with the Church's reaction to it, was hard to bear, but

through it all, I never doubted for a moment that
God still loved me, and that He was on my side.

Karen returned to church after a long gap. How difficult must that have been? And then to arrive and feel like a 'second class citizen', someone who didn't really fit in. Instead of feeling that the church was a sanctuary for her where she could come with her sins and her mistakes and celebrate them as part of our redeemed humanity with the rest of the community of saints, she felt as though she was tolerated; included, but only just. When she later remarried, a prominent member of the congregation was heard to wonder why the minister was marrying someone who had been divorced at all?

It is attitudes like these - experienced by Graham and Karen - that alienate people from the churches. That alienation does much harm. For it is a two-way alienation. People outside the church find that they can no longer hear the good news because the institution that preaches it says it has strings attached. Those of us who are inside find ourselves cut off from these ordinary men and women. We do not know how to speak to them and our response to that fear is to withdraw and be with our own kind. The two stories above show us that even people who are inside the walls of the church may not expect the church to be altogether positive about the choices they are making.

Within Christian congregations up and down the land, and in most countries in the developed world, the ideas surrounding marriage and family will be based on a shaky premise and historical perspective. Many people in the churches will not be married and yet the church will persist in acting as though everyone is or was. Those who do not fit in will either not be there or will be asked to suffer in silence. And if such limited, restricted ideas about the nature of marriage are to form the foundation of family life, God help all of us!

chapter 10

Constancy and covenant

marriage makeover

Changing landscapes

'Family life, on the whole, was pretty stable in middle-class Britain when we were growing up in the late 1940s and 1950s. Issues of sexual orientation and the notion of "being in a relationship" were rarely discussed and divorce, while certainly on the increase, was relatively rare. Marriage, as a natural development of life in your early twenties, was something you expected to enter, just as you took it for granted that you would, at roughly the same time or perhaps a bit earlier, get a job which you could expect to last for life. These expectations were based on the fact - or at least, we assumed it to be a fact - of a stable society within which we would go on living.' (John and Molly Harvey 1997, Page 80)

What a difference a few decades can make! The picture here is of an apparently simpler time and place, where the things that were known were accepted as fixtures and not expected to change. In the Britain of the 1940s and 1950s, many more people lived and worked in the same place than do so today. Their families lived nearby and most of them had some connection with their local church. Fit marriage into this picture and one can see that it has lots of natural supports to help it along. But what price progress?

It seems to me that we have stopped thinking about marriage, and that it has become a victim of that lack of consideration. This means that we no longer truly understand the marriage landscape and that we are trying to impose values from a different era on a generation of people who view and experience the world in a very different way from that of 50 or more years ago. As we saw in the last chapter, some of the key assumptions that underpin our ideas about marriage may well be flawed. That is another reason why we need to look again at what marriage is, and who is allowed to take part in it. We may have thought that the institution of marriage was a constant, a fixed point in the whirling world, but times have changed and we must consider changing too. We must not be afraid, at the very least, to think about new alternatives.

Nowadays the traditional supports of family, community and church are by and large absent - as was said earlier, much has been done to shake the idea of 'the village' that surrounded families in the first half of the twentieth century. Work is something that is no longer the domain of the man as the sole breadwinner; it is something that both partners either wish to or have to participate in.

Society is much more fractured than it once was, and the way we experience work and the way we live can be at odds. At work we may be used to hierarchical structures while at home the relationship between partners is perhaps more equally balanced. A traditional model for marriage might have embraced these words of Paul, 'Wives submit to your husbands as to the Lord. For the husband is the head of the wife as Christ is the head of the church, his body of which he is the Saviour. Now as the church submits to Christ, so also wives should submit to their husbands in everything' (Ephesians 5 22-24; NIV).

This model of the family was hierarchical, and the entire family would probably have engaged in common work, perhaps in agriculture or some kind of service. This shared experience, with the husband at the top of the heap at home and at work, was a powerful and potent way of keeping families together. Today it no longer exists but some sections of church thinking assume that it still does, and even that it is a better way of living.

Today we need a different language for work and home. Both places exist within different sets of assumptions and people need to develop the skills and vocabularies to make sense of the assumptions and to survive in each context.

But where do young couples - both married and pre-married - go to learn these skills? Who can teach them the languages of home and work? Who can help them understand that the person you need to be at work and the person you want to be at home might be two different people? How do we help people who are very focused about their careers and are fuelled by ambition and a desire to succeed (values which our society applauds) to go home to a partner who wants to be treated as an equal and to live with them in mutual regard? 'The growth of individualisation in our society makes it necessary to develop a pattern for one's own life which is often difficult or indeed impossible to combine with partnership' (E Bleske 1998, page 92).

It is precisely because of this that we must all think more about marriage. If it is to remain the ideal relationship of the Christian Church (putting to one side any argument about whether it should have that status or not), then we need to do better in terms of how we understand and support it.

We need to think about how we prepare people for marriage, how our understandings about it are formed in the first place, how we help people through the first faltering steps of living together and how we should support new families. Society is faced with the option of *not* having this discussion and seeing marriage as an institution crumble, or of facing the issues that lie at the heart of current insecurities, working towards a new understanding of what marriage is or might become.

We might start by thinking about why people marry today. It might be convenient to think that it is always because they are in love with their chosen partner and wish to spend the rest of their lives with them, but there are other, possibly less satisfying but still important, reasons:

- People may marry to recreate a lost sense of family. People who have grown up in 'broken homes' are often propelled into relationships which are more about creating something they never had in the first place rather than starting completely afresh with the right person for them.

- People may feel like aliens in a world full of busyness, and the only way they can feel connected is to have that one special person who will root them, help them to define who they are and what they are about.

- People may marry because they just don't want to face life on their own.

- People may marry to have children. The desire to have children, to procreate or to see the 'family name' extended is still very powerful today even if we understand little about it.

- People may marry to get away from the sexual chase! The search for domesticated sex is still an important driving force today.

Perhaps the chances of anyone marrying for what might be considered wholly ideal reasons are small. In today's 'me first' culture, we are all looking for a way of life that best suits our aspirations. Trouble comes when we have to share it with someone else!

Letting in the light

As John and Molly Harvey have said, 'Our understanding of the Christian teaching about marriage ... is being constantly challenged by the experience of people very close to us; we are being driven, again and again, back to the basics of our belief' (Harvey 1997, page 77). They do not suggest that we should launch some kind of 'back to basics' campaign in terms of first principles about marriage - a cheap and easy simplistic morality that is supposed to cover all situations. Instead, they hint at the need to hammer at the walls of what we know until new cracks appear, allowing light through.

And two of the issues in that discussion will have to be how we recognise different types of domestic partnership and how we recognise same-sex couples. And we will have to ask the question, 'Is marriage the monopoly for heterosexual couples or can its blessings and advantages as well as its responsibilities and limits be extended to other groups?'

Today, the church will recognise any marriage between men and women whether it happens inside or outside church. The church has not been afraid to extend its blessing to the marriages of those who do not ask for that blessing in a formal or direct way. A couple who marry in a civil ceremony live in the same state of grace as couples who marry in church. It is clear that the church is very committed to the legal status attached to marriage. And perhaps it is the lack of legal status attached to other forms of committed relationship that makes the church uneasy. Does it beg the question of whether the churches would be happier about other forms of relationship if legal benefits were conferred upon them - as the UK government seems inclined to do?

So if the church will recognise the union of two people in a civil setting, why not give recognition to a man and a woman who choose to commit to one another and live together faithfully, or to a same-sex couple in similar circumstances?

People who choose to live together for a long period of time find that they have some legal protection whether they want it or not. The State now recognises their relationship even if the language used to describe those relationships is still clumsy - how affirming can it be to be called someone's 'common-law wife'? In most cases these days, the church will welcome children of these unions whether for baptism or to join the children's activities.

Things fall apart though when gay and lesbian couples announce that they want the same rights and recognition as everyone else. Then some reactions might suggest that the entire future of the world is uncertain and that if we accede, all understanding of morality will vanish and we will live in an amoral vacuum.

Two key questions are set out for us by Professor Andrew K M Adam in an essay entitled 'Disciples Together, Constantly'. They are: why does God care about our sexual lives? And why do we, as Christian brothers and sisters, care about each other's sexual lives? These questions are very closely linked. Commenting on the work of Adam, D M Matzko points to his understanding of the central theological importance of marriage being 'constancy' and suggests that this points in turn to 'fidelity and hospitality'. Matzko goes on to suggest that this is about an image of God's relationship with the world and Christ's relationship with the church (Matzko 1998).

Alan Richardson says, 'The marriage relationship is the deepest, richest and most satisfying personal relationship of which we have experience: it is an experience of surrender without absorption, of service without compulsion, of love without conditions. In it are illustrated, as far as such divine realities can be illustrated by analogies within human experience, all the truths of God's love and grace' (Alan Richardson 1958, page 258). But is this thing we call marriage, so eloquently described by Richardson, something that can only be experienced within the context of a heterosexual relationship?

Adam argues that 'same-sex unions are not equivalent to heterosexual marriage and the network of goods that make it concrete (e.g. children), but they are able to sustain the fundamental good of constancy'. In fact, Adam suggests that constancy among gay and lesbian couples may provide a more striking image of God's love than many heterosexual unions. Adam has also said, 'The fact that some gay and lesbian Christians have sustained committed relationships over many years, despite the active opposition that such relationships provoke in many quarters, testifies to an admirable and rare sense of constant fidelity. The dignity and integrity of their discipleship are self-evident' (K M Adam 1996 pp129-30).

If marriage is simply about procreation and family - an Augustinian understanding - then its limits are clear. However, if marriage is fundamentally about constancy, if it is about a covenantal relationship between two people, then it is perfectly possible to allow same-sex couples or co-habiting heterosexual couples who can demonstrate these qualities or who have decided they want to, to have their unions recognised.

However, Matzko doesn't want to stop the argument there. 'When Christian theologians make a case for same-sex unions, they usually side-step a consideration of the body, dealing instead with general norms for moral relationships'. So far that is what the churches have done. We have conveniently left out all consideration of what gay and lesbian people do with their bodies for fear of scaring ourselves witless! Matzko goes on to say that, 'any argument for or against same-sex unions in the church needs to attend to the desire of gay and lesbian Christians to make their desires known and to offer their bodies as signs of God's self-giving' (Matzko 1998, p 96). If the churches were to recognise and even bless such unions, then would it not create opportunities to nourish and nurture these relationships, to point people in the direction of God and the Gospel of Jesus Christ?

An argument against recognition might suggest that the basis of marriage is about the *different* sexes coming together and making one flesh. It is about experiencing 'the other' in one's chosen partner. However, Matzko states that homosexual people also 'encounter the other' in persons of the same gender.

These are clearly disturbing and difficult ideas for the church and in raising them here I do not do so lightly. Some people who read this will be incensed; would rather not even think about these issues. Others will wonder what all the fuss is about. If we want to engage in an honest discussion about the possibilities of same-sex marriage, there is already a considerable body of work that will make our journey easier. This is a journey which the church must take if it is to have any integrity in our world. The church must stop standing apart from where people are and how they really live, and join in a genuine search for truth. The conversation is already going on around us - the perception from the outside is that all we can contribute is, 'no!' and 'don't!'

The UK is not the only nation that is struggling with such issues. On a recent trip to Canada it was clear from reading the press that same-sex union was a live issue there. In Canada, public opinion favours same-sex marriage by anything from 53%-64% and support from those aged under 30 is massive. In the last nine years many rights and responsibilities have been extended to same-sex couples, for example, in terms of pensions and adoption. In Canada, according to Margaret Wente of the *Globe and Mail* newspaper, the distinction is not so much between married and non-married as between those in and not in couples.[1]

Writing in the same newspaper, Heather Mallik talks about the response of some of the churches to the idea of recognition for same-sex couples, 'The fundamentalists out on the street with their ketchup-dripping Christ doll are saying that if gays marry and adopt kids, Beelzebub is unleashed.'[2] In June 2003 the Ontario Court of Appeal ruled that denying same-sex couples a civil marriage was unconstitutional, and made its ruling with immediate effect. Similar courts in other parts of Canada had given local legislatures time to frame new laws. The Government of Canada has now made reference to the Supreme Court seeking guidance from them on how it should frame legislation. In the last weeks it has seemingly bowed to pressure from churches to propose a civil union between same-sex couples rather than a civil marriage. However it is clear that Canada has made a huge step - one that has not gone down well with some sections of the Christian community there. Also writing in the *Globe and Mail*, Clive Doucet, Poet and City Councillor in Ottowa, discusses his experience of welcoming the first gay couple to purchase their wedding licence at City Hall. He was happy to report that this event did not result in the sky falling down![3]

In the US, the Episcopal Church has appointed the first openly gay bishop in the Anglican Communion. Bishop Gene Robinson has gone on the record as saying that he can do more for gay and lesbians by being a good bishop rather than being the gay bishop. Writing in the *Los Angeles Times* on August 10 2003, Charlotte Allan suggests that this is another step in the church's prolonged ecclesiastical suicide and that it has

[1] Margaret Wente, 'From the closet to the altar', *Globe and Mail*, Canada, 20 July 2002
[2] Heather Mallik, 'Don't get married, just slit your throat', *Globe and Mail*, Canada, 20 July 2002
[3] *Globe and Mail*, 'You MPs call this a priority'? Clive Doucet, Aug 15 2003

painted itself into 'a corner of trendiness'. She acknowledges that others see the move as a symbol of inclusiveness. This appointment has been met with much anger and frustration from around the Anglican Communion which had just heaved a sigh of relief when Britain's Canon Jeffrey John had decided not to proceed with his ordination as Bishop of Reading. The key issue here is that both these men are in long term stable relationships which have many of the hallmarks of what we would understand as a marriage. Indeed, Jeffrey John has gone on record to say that his relationship has not had a physically sexual dimension for many years, therefore he was living chastely with his long-term partner; which should therefore make his relationship acceptable to those who forbid homosexual practice but 'accept' the homosexual person on the grounds of a chaste lifestyle. And yet his candidacy for Bishop of Reading still could not be accepted because of his sexuality.

Back in the old country, the reaction to Dr Rowan William's appointment as Archbishop of Canterbury echoes this. Before Dr Williams was even in office, voices from a particular wing of the Church of England were expressing grave concerns about his appointment and suggesting that such a man, were he to continue to peddle his 'liberal' ideology, could provoke a split in the Church.

These trends are apparent in Britain and across Europe. In Germany, more than 4000 gay couples have taken advantage of new laws allowing recognition of same-sex relationships.

What is the church to do about this? Maybe we should decide that standing Canute-like against the incoming tide is no longer an option, unless we want to prove that we are irrelevant and redundant. Boswell says, 'One must begin to examine whether toleration of gay sexuality in fact accompanies moral decadence within the Christian community and is associated with the abandonment of Christian ethics in general, or whether it is simply part of a softening of an extreme functionalism in Christian sexual ethics, perhaps within a context of conscientious Christian reform' (Boswell 1980, page 165). The church has to rediscover its mind and use it. It has to be brave and honest, and consider options hitherto believed to be impossible. It has to move away from being a bastion of 'good behaviour' towards becoming the agency of God's grace and generosity.

If the church does not do this then it will lose any influence it has on society and will therefore fail in its mission. It will no longer be salt and light, it will become a museum; a theme park dedicated to a long-distant past; a shadow of what it could have been.

For any understanding of marriage to survive, it needs to be set in the context of life in the twenty-first century and the way human beings choose to live. Struggling for that understanding cannot be about trying to control how people behave; instead it must be about recognising that when two people - of whatever combination - choose to commit to one another, the church as well as the state should be there to welcome that union, and to support them when they say 'I do'.

chapter 11

Learning the lingo

It is always surprising when lifestyle commentators tell us that we live in a 'values-free' age. Nothing could be further from the truth. Values - beliefs and ideas that we consider to be important - invade all aspects of life. However, the problem with values is that they are often provisional and portable. In a previous age, the values attached to marriage made it virtually the only relationship choice. As a result, it helped to maintain relationships that were sometimes clearly and indisputably abusive. Now values have changed. Women have more of a voice and a greater measure of equality, and as a result they are valued more and violence against them is now considered unacceptable by most people.

Values change, all the time. In previous generations a child born out of wedlock might routinely be considered, and called, a 'bastard'. In today's world such terminology is considered offensive and irrelevant. However, it is folly to believe that all the values we live with today will survive into the next generation. We all need to be comfortable with the idea of changing values. Having been involved with the churches for nearly 20 years my sense is that this is often the last place where such comfort can be found! And therein lies the problem. The church no longer lives in real time. For many members, the church has become the last bastion, the last defence against the invasion of that apparently 'values-free morality'. It exists to point to a better day, a better age, a more human time. It points to a rich history, a glorious heritage, an enduring tradition. However, it often does little to enrich or enlighten the present.

For many reasons the churches need to rediscover their original purpose. I am personally very tired of well-worn clichés such as, 'The church is the only institution which exists not for itself'. (That's one of my favourites.) It sounds good, but implausible; like a lovely fairy-tale.

Whatever God intended for the church, the reality is that we aren't anywhere near that now. It's time for us to make a clear choice. We need to create a place where we can connect with the world as it is, and not as we would like it to be. A place where we can learn a new language.

In the many months I have been writing about these issues I have been amazed by the number of people I have met who have told me how the church has hurt them. How it has punished them for their sexual 'misbehaviour'. If I had included all their stories then this book would have been considerably longer.

Conclusion

My conclusion is that the salvation of the church will happen only if it learns a new language; and the nature of this language will be:

- The language of respect
- The language of identity
- The language of inclusion and welcome
- The language of wholeness
- The language of intimacy

If we do this, not only will the church be saved from a pointless existence and a shaky future, it will regain its power to be a force for salvation. It will become an agent for change at all levels of our society but most importantly in the hearts of the people.

It is worth looking again at Jesus' encounter with the Samaritan woman that we find in John 4.

The woman at the well

So Jesus left the Judean countryside and went back to Galilee. To get there he had to pass through a Samaritan village that bordered the field Jacob had given his son Joseph. Jacob's well was still there. Jesus, worn out by the journey, sat down at the well. It was noon.

A woman, a Samaritan, came to draw water. Jesus said, 'would you give me a drink of water?' (His disciples had gone to the village to buy food for lunch.)

The Samaritan woman, taken aback, asked, 'How come you, a Jew, are asking me, a Samaritan woman, for a drink?' (Jews in those days wouldn't be caught dead talking to Samaritans.)

Jesus answered, 'If you knew the generosity of God and who I am, you would be asking me for a drink and I would give you fresh, living water.'

The woman said, 'Sir, you don't even have a bucket to draw with, and this well is deep. So how are you going to get this 'living water'? Are you a better man than our ancestor Jacob, who dug this well and drank from it, he and his sons and livestock, and passed it down to us?'

Jesus said, 'Everyone who drinks this water will get thirsty again and again. Anyone who drinks the water I give will never thirst - not ever. The water I give will be a spring within, gushing fountains of endless life.'

(John 4, taken from The Message, *Eugene Peterson)*

What an amazing encounter this is. It lays the foundation for an understanding of what learning a new language might mean for us.

In his encounter with this most 'fallen' of women, Jesus did not run away from her or condemn her. Instead, he showed her respect in a way that possibly no man ever had. His behaviour would certainly have been considered strange by anyone who saw it. She was a harlot and a Samaritan! Why would the King of Kings and Lord of Lords waste his time with her? Perhaps he knew that at some point far in the future, his church would be so alienated from ordinary people that this story, one that would stand the test of time, would be needed as an example and a reminder of the generosity and respect of God.

Jesus recognised this woman. He knew exactly who and what she was. He knew what she had done and why. Her willing acceptance of the water of life and her subsequent rush to share the good news is clear evidence of that. He knew who he was dealing with and he was not afraid to be with her. To stand with someone so different from himself and yet to offer that person his own riches.

Jesus offered the woman a place at his table. He did not exclude her because of her gender, her ethnic identity or her sexual activities. Instead he offered her the greatest gift of all - and she the first in all her village. She was welcome. She was included. Jesus said so.

Jesus offered the woman wholeness and well-being. He told her that if she let him satisfy her thirst then she would never thirst again. He convinced her - and that in itself is a miracle, for such a woman must have had a fairly cynical view of men. And yet this man was different. There was something about him ... Oh, that people could say that of the church and the people in it.

Jesus used the language of intimacy with this woman surprisingly quickly. He allowed her to parry his questions - in some senses it was as though he was flirting with her, wooing her until suddenly she was standing in a place she had never seen before. A place she had never expected to be.

Breaking down walls

Our world today is full of people who do not know any intimacy, and as a result they damage themselves and the people and communities around them. Genuine, unconditional intimacy is one of the most powerful forces available to us in the church and yet we act as though there is only a limited amount available. We put the largest part of it aside for safe keeping and share a meagre amount amongst ourselves, leaving little for people 'outside'. And so we belong to emaciated churches, whose lack of intimacy confirms the worst suspicions of the 'faithful and honest sinner' - that the church is no place for them. 'Our churches are filled with people who outwardly look contented and at peace but inwardly are crying out for someone to love them... just as they are - confused, frustrated, frightened, guilty, and often unable to communicate even within their own families. But the other people in the church look so happy and contented that one seldom has the courage to admit his own deep needs before such a self-sufficient group as the average church meeting appears to be.'[1]

[1] Keith Miller as quoted in Howard Snyder 1975, p90

Who wants to be part of a church like that? Why would one swap the freedom one might feel to explore God outside the structures of the institutional churches for the chains and shackles of such an experience of congregational life?

Looking to a secular model

Community Education Validation and Endorsement (CeVe) is the agency empowered by the Scottish Executive through Communities Scotland to ensure proper standards in the training and delivery of community education services in Scotland. As a new profession, Community Educators have had to think about who they are and what they are supposed to offer.

In 1995, CeVe came up with a clear statement of important principles that should underpin good practice in working with people in the community:

- Respect the individual and their right to self-determination

- Respect and value pluralism

- Value equality

- Encourage collective action

- Promote lifelong learning

- Encourage participation

(*Guidelines for Pre-Qualifying Training*, CeVe, Edinburgh, 1995)

How some church people struggle with this list. How resistant some of them can be to principles such as equality and respect! This set of principles demonstrates the new language the church needs to learn. Respect, identity, inclusion, welcome, wholeness, and intimacy.

When I see this list, I think about God. I think about the people I know who feel excluded from the church and in this list I see hope that one day they might have a place at the table. Or that they might take the place they already have. The church needs to respect every human life as though it were made in the image of God. Even if that life represents something different from what it regards as the 'norm'; even if it appears threatening. This should be non-negotiable.

There are single people in our churches who are quietly desperate because they are seen only as fodder for Sunday School or for baby-sitting, or are pitied because they are 'on the shelf'. Sometimes they are even told to hurry up and get married! In treating single people this way, the church shows insensitivity to the possibility that being single is a state brought about through difficult and painful circumstances. It also shows ignorance of the fact that for many people today singleness is a choice freely made. It is not necessarily about the absence of something but about the presence of something. Some single people will choose to be celibate and some will not. Celibacy has often been described as the 'gift nobody wants'. We need to talk about it more often and to recognise it as another, normal, lifestyle choice. It is not in the church's gift to decide who is 'deserving' and 'undeserving' in this area. All are worthy of equal respect. Unconditional grace. The generosity of God.

Another area for new language concerns people in the church who are childless. Some don't want to be, others are very happy not having children, yet those in both categories may feel patronised by the image of the 'perfect nuclear family' that the church has held up as the ideal.

When I work with students, there are usually some who cannot cope with these ideas and this always strikes me as strange. Why should people who are single or childless seem to threaten their stability? Pluralism is seen as a dark and dangerous thing! Equality can go too far! Collective action and participation might end up in the empowerment of ordinary people which could damage the very firmament on which the church stands - or so it seems.

So what do we do? First, perhaps, we need to reclaim the Bible.

The Bible as a contemporary text

The Bible is a confusing book. At times it seems to give us clear guidance on how we should live and at others it just doesn't. If the Bible were clear about the issues of sexuality then it is unlikely there would be so many arguments about it raging in the churches today! However, the important point to consider here is the place of the Bible in this discussion - it is a key resource book and one which can be used positively to help people understand what sexuality is and how to live with it responsibly. It may no longer be possible to use it as a 'rule book' from which the churches utter the commands of God.'

(Steve Mallon 2002, page 143)

It is no longer legitimate to use the Bible to exclude people who 'misbehave'. That is not the way of love or grace. Nor is it the proper way to exercise judgement or discernment. Boswell points this out very clearly:

...it is important to bear in mind in this context that the same fathers of the church - a very vocal minority - who censured homosexual behaviour also censured, no less severely, behaviour which is today universally accepted by Christian communities. Lending at interest, sexual intercourse during the menstrual period, jewellery or dyed fabrics, shaving, regular bathing, wearing wigs, serving in the civil government or army, performing manual labour on feast days, eating kosher food, practising circumcision - all were condemned absolutely by various fathers of the church, the same who condemned homosexual behaviour and many other activities, due to personal prejudice, misinformation, or an extremely literal interpretation of the Bible. None of these practices is today a matter of controversy within the Christian community, and it seems illogical to claim that it was the opposition of a few influential Christian theorists which caused homosexual practices alone, out of hundreds of proscribed actions, to incur such a powerful and permanent stigma in Western culture. Obviously some more sophisticated analysis is required.

(Boswell 1980, page 165)

There are so many inconsistencies in the way we choose to interpret the Scriptures today that if we choose to make an exception on this particular issue, we limit ourselves and God's grace.

It is no longer legitimate to pretend that the Bible suggests that only one form of relationship, marriage, is valid. The Bible reports on a variety of relationships between many different types of people and a great many of these relationships were entirely dysfunctional. Would we use King David as a role model for marriage? Definitely not, but we can use him as a role model for a three-dimensional person of faith who knew when he had made a mess of his life and who somehow stayed connected to his idea of God.

It is time to reclaim the Bible as a book which can inspire confidence in offering to those who cannot or will not be part of our communities, the grace and salvation of God - and indeed to ourselves - regardless of who we all are and what we do. Our underlying premise must be that all are made in the image of God and worthy of our respect.

It is time to reclaim the Bible as the source-book for defining our responsibilities to ourselves and to one another. It is clear that in human life there are times when we need boundaries, and suggestions for these boundaries are given to us in the Scriptures. That we consider how we might apply them for today does not mean we are abandoning God or disregarding the intentions of the Scripture writers. Rather, we are living up to the idea that Jesus is the 'eternal contemporary', and we are exercising our minds and hearts to consider what he is saying today.

It is time for the church to use the Bible as the dictionary for the new language of inclusion and welcome, for the language of respect and generosity. This does not mean that we will introduce a free-for-all approach - far from it. It will help us define our responsibilities to one another; consider how best to meet them and how to work together when we are in conflict.

It is time for us to rediscover the power of truth. It cannot be fully contained on paper between two covers. It cannot be fully contained in human minds and hearts. Truth is alive and is a wild and awesome thing. It does not rest or linger in one place for too long. We cannot domesticate it. Truth always will out, but when that happens, do we in the church ignore it?

It is time for us to accept that there are people in our world who live differently, not as we in the churches might hope they would. Our ideals for human relationships - while valid in some respects - may not be shared by all or even a majority of people. To respond by making more distance between ourselves and the 'badly behaved' makes no sense. We are now an estranged church, far too distant from the people we are supposed to engage with.

There are people in our churches who are gay. There are people who are single. There are people who are in good and in bad marriages. There are people who are childless by choice, or who desperately want children. There are people who are divorced or bereaved, who struggle with loneliness. All of this is about sexuality. All of this is about salvation.

It's time for churches that can be positive to come out of the closet and make their intentions known. Where can young, gay Christians go to church? Where are the churches that will welcome divorced people and not make them feel a failure? Where are the churches that will be honest about sexuality to those who are married and to those embarking on the journey of marriage or of living together? Somehow these churches need to make more noise, because in this new millennium these are the churches that will grow.

In the last decade, the biggest growth in church life in the UK was in the evangelical and charismatic sectors. Many disaffected members of institutional churches have found in these churches a better experience of worship, better preaching and a warmer welcome. As the institutional churches have declined, so these free churches have grown and this trend will probably continue. However it is likely that their chief source of new members will be from other churches rather than from raw recruits. The churches that will grow organically in the next few years will be those who place an emphasis on community, family (in its broadest sense) and inclusion. They will be robustly Christian and orthodox but will agree to agree on the essentials and argue about everything else in a constructive, holy and useful way. These are churches where the language will be one of respect and where no question will be too stupid to ask.

In the United States, some Presbyterian churches identify themselves as 'more light' churches. This means that those congregations are positive about diversity. The explicit aim of these churches is to '...seek the full participation of lesbian, gay, bisexual and transgendered people of faith in the life, ministry and witness of the Presbyterian Church (USA)'. The interesting thing about this organization is that it is a congregation-by-congregation association. It is sizeable in nature and clearly makes its aims known within the structures of the denomination. Its strength comes in the fact that it journeys within the Presbyterian Church and not from outside. Perhaps a similar movement is required in the UK?[2]

In this new century, the churches that grow will be those that speak a new language. Churches that offer a place of comfort, solace and challenge to those who have 'misbehaved' and feel they do not fit in. Churches that will not peddle absolute certainty but will leave room for doubt. Churches that understand what salvation must mean to someone who is gay or single or divorced or married or old or young. Churches that will offer that salvation to the church in exile - the people wandering in the desert. And in so doing, these churches will themselves find salvation.

[2] For information on More Light Churches go to www.mlp.org

Epilogue - The Vision

About noon the following day as they were on their journey and approaching the city, Peter went up on the roof to pray. He became hungry and wanted something to eat, and while the meal was being prepared, he fell into a trance. He saw heaven opened and something like a large sheet being let down to earth by its four corners. It contained all kinds of four-footed animals, as well as reptiles of the earth and birds of the air. Then a voice told him, 'Get up, Peter. Kill and eat.'

'Surely not, Lord!' Peter replied. 'I have never eaten anything impure or unclean.' The voice spoke to him a second time, 'Do not call anything impure that God has made clean.' This happened three times, and immediately the sheet was taken back to heaven.

Acts 10:9-16 (NIV)

This is an incredible passage of Scripture and gives us a good place to end our conversation.

Peter had moved from being a man full of uncertainties to a man living with certainty. He knew who he was, he knew who Jesus really was. He knew where he was standing and why. I think he thought he was finished, that he was complete. God, it seems, had other plans.

For Peter to be told to eat what appeared on the blanket in front of him was not just unusual, it was offensive and frankly horrific. Peter was a good Jew. He would never have eaten any of those things. And yet now God seemed to be telling him to go ahead and do just that. This is fantastic! We cannot comprehend just how mad this must have seemed to Peter. God was pushing him beyond his comfort-zones to make a point.

God is doing the same to us today.

'Do not call anything impure that God has made clean,' is the response God gave to Peter. Without this encounter, Peter might have missed the opportunity to see that God was operating outside the boundaries in which Peter was happy to live. He would have missed the fact that the still-faltering church was about to make another evolutionary leap. He was about to learn that Jesus had not just died for the Jews but had died for everyone. And yet he could have so easily believed the opposite without that divine intervention.

What of us today? Does the church represent Peter before or after this revelation? Do we see some people as unclean and therefore presume that they are beyond the love, grace, mercy and judgement of God?

I work with lots of gay, lesbian and bisexual people today - all of them Christians. It's hard for those who have not experienced it to understand the power and privilege of witnessing the moment when they can just be open about their sexuality and know that no-one will jump down their throats; when they know that their acceptance is guaranteed, that the love surrounding them is truly unconditional. And I've seen how that moment has helped many heterosexual young people become more open about their sexuality too, giving them a context in which they can better understand themselves and better integrate their faith with their sexuality.

This can only be a good thing. The churches need to see that God is doing this kind of thing with people all over the world. God is helping us make safe spaces for people to talk about sex, faith and relationships without fear of censure. At the moment this is happening outside the boundaries of the churches - sometimes with their tacit approval - but it is time that the boundaries were enlarged and that we heard the divine words say once more, 'Do not call anything impure that God has made clean.'

It interests me that Peter denied his Lord three times and then in that great moment of reconciliation told Jesus that he loved him three times. In this chapter Peter has to be reminded three times that he is called not just to love the Lord but his fellow man.

We need to go and do likewise.

To those of us who deem ourselves to be liberal, we cannot deny verses in the Scriptures that trouble and seem to prohibit the humanity of some of our brothers and sisters. We must talk about these things and we must not demonise those who genuinely believe these scriptures to be true. To those of us who deem ourselves to be conservative, we must not use these scriptures to divide and exclude. These are not attributes that fit well with the mission of the church.

All of us have to ask ourselves this question honestly: Do we really believe that, if the Bible did not have the very few references it has to homosexuality contained within it, gay and lesbian people would fare any better?

This is who we are. We cannot deny ourselves. We are a curious and wonderful people made up of men and women, young and old, from different races and places. People who are rich and poor. People who are gay, straight, single, married, living with a partner, in families, childless, celibate, sexually active, and on it goes. This is who we are. And all are welcome in God's house.

To finish, here's a quote that sums up this whole situation for me. It's written by Eleanor Roosevelt. I have no idea where I read it, but it is something that I go back to again and again for inspiration. Let it inspire you to make the church better at being human and divine. Let it inspire us all to find salvation for ourselves - but not before we offer it to those we might otherwise consider to be unclean.

'Where after all do human rights begin? In small places, close to home - so close and so small they cannot be seen on any maps of the world. Yet they are the world of the individual person; the neighbourhood he lives in; the school or college he attends; the factory, farm or office where he works. Such are the places where every man, woman and child seeks equal justice, equal opportunity, equal dignity without discrimination.

Unless these rights have meaning there, they have little meaning anywhere. Without concerted citizen action to uphold them close to home, we shall look in vain for progress in the larger world.'

We need to act. Now is the time. Today is the day of salvation.
Amen.

Steve Mallon

Chapter

study guide

It became clear while writing this book that the emphasis on conversations about sexuality and developing a vocabulary to assist these were going to be the dominant themes. With this in mind, it seemed like a good idea to have this study guide available to readers to use either individually or in small groups. The hope is that this will make the book a practical one, one that will get people thinking and talking; these are the only tools we have if we are to challenge any resistance to change. They may not seem like much but in fact, they are all we need.

The study guide has an opening reflection to get you into the swing of things and then follows with sections relating firstly to the introduction and then to each subsequent chapter. The emphasis is on reflection and reaction. Your own stories are important here, but always take care on how and to whom you tell them. If you are meeting with a group, then make sure your group agrees absolute confidentiality before you work through the study guide.

I hope you find using the study guide helpful. Learning is a funny thing - we engage in it and yet at the same time it often simply happens to us. We think we can control it, and yet we are often at its mercy. I hope you learn a lot as you work through these pages.

1: A place to begin

Reflection

On your own or as a group think about the quote from Martin Luther King Jr that appears on page i:

'Our lives begin to end the day we become silent about things that matter.'

- Why is it important not to be silent about sexuality within the context of the Christian faith?

- Why do you think that it is so difficult to talk about issues relating to sexuality?

- What can we do about that? In our local churches? On a wider scale?

Activity

If you are comfortable, discuss with a partner the story of your own sexual awakening.
- What happened to make you notice that things were changing?

- Who did you speak to?

- How helpful were they?

- If you could speak to your adolescent self now what message would you give to yourself?

- How easy or uncomfortable do you feel about discussing your sexual story?

2: Focus on the Introduction

Reflection

- Do you think it is wrong for same-sex couples to adopt children? What do you think forms your opinion?

- Do you have a different view in terms of unmarried heterosexual couples adopting children? If so, what explains the different perspectives?

- How has the discussion about sexuality and family developed since you were young? What is good about the change and what do you find difficult?

- Where do you think the churches should be in these discussions? What is the churches' role?

Action

Read again the extract from the Evening Times article at the beginning of this chapter. Read it out loud to yourself or in a group.

- If you were in a stable, committed and long-term relationship, either with someone of the same sex or in an unmarried context, how might this article make you feel?

- If you were someone who was already struggling to reconcile your sexuality and your spirituality, would the position taken by these key religious leaders help you in your quest?

- Did the religious leaders do the right thing? Is it the role of religion to set limits on what is and what is not acceptable in terms of sexuality and family?

3: Focus on Chapter One

Reflection

There are two stories at the beginning of this chapter. One a young man who finds himself in his mid-twenties without ever having had a real sexual experience and the other a woman in her thirties in the process of splitting up from her husband.

Pick one of these stories and try to put yourself into the position of the people involved.

- How does that feel?
- What are your options?
- How might you see God?
- How might you see the church?

Action

In this chapter it is asserted that the churches need to be saved from irrelevance and that one of the ways forward might be for it to change its attitudes to people and their sexualities.

Do you agree with this?

Think about your own church or fellowship group. How welcoming is it to people in the following categories:

- Single parents
- Divorced men and women
- Elderly widowed
- Gay men and lesbians
- Young couples living together

Is there a sense in which the church decides that some groups deserve sympathy while others deserve less? If so, who decides?

4: Focus on Chapter Two

Reflection

This chapter focuses on sex education in schools.

Think about when you first heard 'the facts of life':

- Who was it that told you and where?
- What did you think at the time?
- Did you talk to your peer group?
- If so did you get contradictory information from them?

Do you think there should be an emphasis on relationship education rather than just sex education? If so, how can the church complement that?

Action

If a young woman who was a member of your youth fellowship discovered she was pregnant would she turn to:

- The minister or pastor
- The youth worker
- A friend in the youth fellowship
- Another church member
- Someone outside the church

- Why would she pick the person you've chosen?
- If you said that she would pick someone outside the church; why do you think that is?
- How can we make our churches places where people can share their sexual misadventures and receive support, love and forgiveness?

5: Focus on Chapter Three

Reflection

- Why do you think that marriage is less popular than it was in previous generations?

- Why do you think so many marriages end in divorce?

This chapter discusses the idea of the 'village' concept where we all have a sense of responsibility for one another.

How well would you rate your own 'village'? What are its strengths and weaknesses? Who is in your 'village'?

Action

In Scotland people are becoming more relaxed and liberal about different expressions of sexuality. There are many in the churches who would not wish to be identified with this liberalisation.

- What should the churches' position be on homophobia? (Where gay and lesbian people experience direct or indirect discrimination because of their sexuality.)

- What would Jesus have to say about this situation and how might He deal with it?

6: Focus on Chapter Four

Reflection

Why is it that we are seeing such increases in the incidence of STIs (sexually transmitted infections) in the UK? What do you think are the underlying causes:

- Poor education?

- Bad moral choices?

- Lack of information?

- Consumption of alcohol?

- The way in which discussion about sexuality is kept hidden?

- When you were reading through the sections on STIs, what was going through your mind?

- If God really did invent sex, why are the churches always telling people to stay away from it?

- How can the church celebrate sex as an act, and as a way of being human?

Action

- How can the church help to go beyond the stereotyped responses that follow publication of the kind of statistics we see in this chapter?

- How do we help the young people in our youth fellowships and other youth organisations to have a healthy attitude to sex and sexuality and thereby help them to make good sexual choices?

- If that's not happening in your church now, how will you make it happen?

7: Focus on Chapter Five

Reflection

Have you experienced times when your sexual choices have been in conflict with the expectations you believe your faith and church impose upon you? If so, how did you resolve the conflict?

If you can't answer that question, is there someone else you know that serves as an example?

Put yourself in the position of a young gay man aged 16 who is a member of your church. He is devout in his faith and yet his adolescence is in full flow and he knows that he is gay.

- What options does he have in relation to your church?

- Who can he talk to?

- If he chooses to express his sexuality will he be able to stay in your church or might he have to leave?

Action

Read again the quote from the Sean Gill book, and the *Scotland on Sunday* quote relating to Cardinal Thomas Winning.

These quotes set out the sense of struggle, and the response from one individual in the church.

- If the young man quoted by Sean Gill was in your church, what would he hear from you?

- When you read the statistics about gay and lesbian people feeling harassed or experiencing violence in churches, what is your reaction?

- What should happen to eliminate this?

8: Focus on Chapter Six

Reflection

There are a lot of statistics given in this chapter. Pick one you find interesting, and discuss it with your group or reflect on it on your own.

Do any of the statistics surprise you?

- Do you agree that the difference in the responses offered by the young people does suggest that attitudes in the church might change over time? Do you think this is a good thing - or further evidence of the churches' decline into a moral anachronism?

- If your minister or pastor were to offer support to an openly gay or lesbian young person, do you think s/he would be criticised or challenged by other people in the church?

Action

Take time to talk to some people in your fellowship using the same questions used in this chapter to see what your own church's answers might be. When you have the results, ask yourself what they tell you about your fellowship.

9: Focus on Chapter Seven

Reflection

'I think I convinced myself that [my sexuality] was wrong, but at the bottom of my heart I thought, this can't be wrong. How come if we are all created by this God then why am I like this? I didn't choose this way.' (Robert).

- If Robert had just said this to you how would you respond?

- Put yourself in his position and think about how your response might impact on him. Would it help him or not?

Action

On page 58 we saw that the marks of an inclusive community are:

- Integration

- Prevention

- Understanding

- Inclusiveness

- Empowerment

Think about the following groups, and ask how inclusive your fellowship is:

- Single men and women

- Divorced men and women

- Single parents

- Elderly housebound

- People with disabilities

What kind of work does your church need to do if it is to call itself 'inclusive'? What has it already achieved?

10: Focus on Chapter Eight

Reflection

Have you ever heard someone use the phrase, 'hate the sin, love the sinner'?

- What does this phrase really mean?

- How can someone hate part of you and yet say they love you?

- Does this mean that God hates part of us?

- If Jesus has died to forgive our sins what is left to hate?

Action

Look at the list of suggestions for change that have been formulated by young people and appear in this chapter.

- Which of the suggestions do you think you could implement in your church and which do you think could not be implemented?

- What steps would you take to implement the changes you feel you can make?

11: Focus on Chapter Nine

Reflection

'We live with what we know, and the churches know marriage.' (Page 69)

- Why is it that the churches are sometimes afraid to consider other forms of long term commitment between people?

- Can the churches still hold on to the 'ideal of marriage', when so many marriages fail and so many people choose to live together without getting married?

- Does this change suggest the churches need to change their position to one that might be considered to be more 'inclusive'?

Action

- What can your church do to support young couples who present themselves for marriage? How can the church help them to prepare?

- What shape should such preparations take? What kind of commitment would be required from the couples? If they refused to take part would you prevent them from being married in your church?

- How can we support those who are already married and who may be struggling to stay faithful?

- How do we support those whose marriages have failed and feel incredibly guilty and angry?

12: Focus on Chapter Ten

Reflection

It is suggested in this chapter that we have stopped thinking about marriage. If so, then how can we kick-start a new conversation about it?

Read the quote from John and Molly Harvey that begins, 'Our understanding of the Christian teaching about marriage…' (page 79). They suggest that their understanding is shaped and reformed by the experiences of those around them.

   Think about people you know, and their experiences. Do they offer insights for you into the ideal of marriage? If not, what does the Gospel of Jesus Christ have to say to them?

Action

- Do you agree that the state should recognise same-sex partnerships, as is the case in many other countries in Europe and in North America?

- If such legislation were introduced in the UK what might the reaction be?

- What practical case can be made for this change?

- What is the case against?

13: Focus on Chapter Eleven

Reflection

Read again the suggestion made for the new language that will enable new conversations to happen about sex and sexuality (page 84).

The assertion is made that learning this language will not only offer healing to those around us but to the church itself.

Do you agree with this idea in full or in part? Do you have a sense of disconnection between the church and the wider community? If so, how might this language help to make a reconnection?

Action

The story of Jesus and his encounter with the woman at the well is remarkable in many respects.

Think of someone you know - it might even be yourself - whose life has fallen short in the eyes of the wider community and play out this story between Jesus and that person.

- How does the story go?
- How does it finish?
- Is it a happy ending?

References and Further Reading

Introduction

I have been writing about these issues for 5 years now and have used many publications from a wide variety of sources. Any incorrect information listed against any source of material is purely mine and I crave everyone's forgiveness.

The list which follows shows some of the books and sources that were used in the writing of *Sexuality and Salvation* together with other resources that will be helpful to any reader who wishes to take these issues further.

Books

Adam K M, 1996, 'Disciples Together Constantly' from Choon-Leong Seow (ed), 1996, *Homosexuality and Christian Community*, Louisville, Westminster/John Knox Press

Altman D, 1983, *The Homosexualisation of America*, Boston, Beacon Press

Bell J, 1993, *Doing Your Research Project* (2nd Ed), Buckingham, Open University Press

Boisvert D L, 2000, *Out on Holy Ground: Meditations on Gay Men's Spirituality*, Cleveland, The Pilgrim Press

Boswell J, 1980, *Christianity, Social Tolerance and Homosexuality*, Chicago, University of Chicago Press

Byrne D, 1999, *Social Exclusion*, Buckingham, Open University Press

Capon R, 1982, *Between Noon and Three*, New York, Harper and Row

Clinton H R, 1996, *It Takes a Village*, New York, Simon and Schuster

Denniston J, 2003, 'The Last Taboo' from Steve Mallon (Ed) *Inside Verdict: A Changing Church in a Changing Scotland*, Edinburgh, Scottish Christian Press

Empereur J L, 1998, *Spiritual Direction and the Gay Person*, New York, Continuum Publishing

Epstein D, Johnson R, 1998, *Schooling Sexualities*, Buckingham, Open University Press

Epstein D, O' Flynn S, Telford D, *Silenced Sexualities in Schools and Universities*, Stoke on Trent, Trentham Books

Friend R, 1993, 'Choices not Closets: Heterosexism and Homophobia in Schools' from Weiss and Fine (Eds), *Beyond Silenced Voices: Class, Race and Gender in United States Schools*, Albany, State University of New York Press

Gill S, 1988, *Lesbian and Gay Christian Movement*, London, Cassell

Haralambros M, Holborn M, 1995, *Sociology: Themes and Perspectives* (4th Ed), London, Collins Educational

Harvey J and M, 1997, 'For the Rest of Your Life' from Galloway K (Ed), *Dreaming of Eden*, Glasgow, Wild Goose Publications

Hawkes G, 1996, *A Sociology of Sex and Sexuality*, Buckingham, Open University Press

Hill M, Tisdall K, 1997, *Children and Society*, London, Longman Higher Education

Jones G, 1995, *Organisational Theory: Text and Cases*, Boston, Addison-Wesley Publishing

Kendal R T, 1988, *Is God for the Homosexual?*, Basingstoke, Marshall Pickering

Kent-Baguley P, 1990, 'Working with Gay and Lesbian Young People' from Jeffs T and Smith M (Eds) *Young People, Inequality and Youth Work*, Basingstoke, Macmillan Press

Koteskey R L, 1991, *Psychology from a Christian Perspective*, Lanham, Rowman & Littlefield

McCall Tigert L & Brown T, 2001, *Coming Out Young and Faithful*, Cleveland, The Pilgrim Press

Neuman W, 1997, *Social Research Methods*, Allyn & Bacon

Owens R E, 1998, *Queer Kids: The Challenges and Promise for Lesbian, Gay and Bisexual Youth*, Binghamton, The Hawthorn Press

Phipps W E, 1996, *The Sexuality of Jesus*, Cleveland, The Pilgrim Press

Ramafedi G, 1994, *Death by Denial: Studies of Gay and Lesbian Suicide*, Boston, Alyson Publications

Richardson A, 1958, *An Introduction to the Theology of the New Testament*, London, SCM Press

Robson C, 1993, *Real World Research*, Oxford, Blackwell

Rudy K, 1997, *Sex and the Church*, Boston, Beacon Press

Silverman D, *The Theory of Organisations*, London, Heinemann

Singer, 1993, 'Breaking Through' Rochester Democrat and Chronicle as quoted in Owens R E, 1998, *Queer Kids: The Challenges and Promise for Lesbian, Gay and Bisexual Youth*, Binghamton, The Hawthorn Press

Sullivan A, 1996, *Virtually Normal*, London, Picador

Vasey M, 1995, *Strangers and Friends: A new Exploration of Homosexuality and the Bible*, London, Hodder and Staughton

Yaconelli M, 2002, *Messy Spirituality*, London, Hodder Christian Books

Journal Articles

Benson J K, 1977, 'Organisations: A Dilectical View' from *Administrative Science Quarterly Review*, Volume 22

Langeveld M J, 1965, 'In Search of Research' *Paedigogical Europoea*, Volume I

Loranger M, 1997, 'The Need to Belong', from *The Spirituality of Young People - The Way Supplement*, 1997/90

Mallon S, 2002, 'Developing a Positive Sexuality Education in the Churches' from *British Journal of Theological Education*, Volume 12.2

Matzko D M, 1998, 'The Relationship of Bodies', *Journal of Theology and Sexuality*, Number 8

Petrovic J E, 2000, 'Caring Without Justice' from *International Journal of Children's Spirituality*, Volume 5 Number 1

Thatcher A, 1998, 'Crying out for Discernment', *Journal of Theology and Sexuality*, Number 8

Yip A K T, 1998, 'Gay Male Christians' Perspective of the Christian Community in Relation to their Sexuality' from *Journal of Theology and Sexuality*, Number 8

Organisational Documents

Church of Scotland, 1994, *Human Sexuality*, report to the 1994 General Assembly of the Church of Scotland, Edinburgh, Board of Practice and Procedure

Community Education Validation and Endorsement, 1995, *Guidelines for Pre-qualifying Training*, Edinburgh, CeVe

Greater Glasgow Health Board, 2002, *Something to Tell you - A Health Needs Assessment of Young Gay, Lesbian and Bisexual Young People in Glasgow*, Glasgow, GGHB

United Nations, 1993, *The Rights of the Child, Guide to the UN Convention*, Department of Health and Children's Rights Development Unit

Office for National Statistics, 2002, Fifty Years of Change

Terrence Higgins Trust, Autumn Newsletter 1999

Internet Resources

The Church of England's View on Issues of Human Sexuality,
http://www.cofe.anglican.org/view/sexuality.html

Anthony Giddens, Runaway World, Reith Lectures 1999,
http://www.lse.ac.uk/Giddens/reith_99/

PCUSA Polity Reflections Note 42, Constitutional Status of Ceremonies Blessing Same-Sex Relationships, March 2001
http://horeb.pcusa.org/oga/PolityReflections/Note42.htm

Other Media

Mallik H, 2002, 'Don't Get Married, Just Slit Your Throat', *Globe and Mail,* Toronto

Wente M, 2002, 'From the Closet to the Altar', *Globe and Mail,* Toronto

Useful sources of information

BBC - *www.bbc.co.uk/health/sex*

British Society of Gerontology - *www.britishgerontology.org*

Christian Institute - *www.christian.org.uk*

Church of Scotland 'Church without walls' - *www.churchwithoutwalls.org.uk*

Church of Scotland - *www.churchofscotland.org.uk*

Greenbelt Festival - *www.greenbelt.org.uk*

Health Education Board for Scotland HEBS - *www.hebs.com*

Healthy Respect - *www.healthy-respect.com*

LGBT Youth Scotland - *www.lgbtyouth.org.uk*

Public Health Laboratory Service, information now available at -
   www.hpa.org.uk/infections/default.htm

Religious Tolerance - *www.religioustolerance.org*

Roman Catholic Church in Scotland - *www.catholic-scotland.org.uk*

Stonewall - *www.stonewall.org.uk*

Terrance Higgins Trust - *www.tht.org.uk*

Care for the Family - *www.care-for-the-family.org.uk*

The Place - *www.theplace-sandyford.co.uk*

Scottish Equality Network - *www.equality-network.org*

Strathclyde Lesbian and Gay Switchboard - 0141 847 0447

National Lesbian and Gay Switchboard - 020 7837 7324 (24 hrs)

Lesbian and Gay Christian Counselling Helpline - 020 7739 8134

Lothian Gay and Lesbian Switchboard - 0131 556 4049

Sexual Health and National AIDS Helpline - 0800 567123

Childline - 0800 1111

Women's Aid - 08457 023 468 - *www.womensaid.org.uk*

NCH - *www.nch.org.uk* - good resources for children and young people

These numbers and addresses were correct at the time of going to print 19/01/04.